Endo

"Nossokoff captures the drama of sacrificial humanitarian work, reveals the hearts of humble servants, and inspires readers. *Faith Alive: Stories of Hope and Healing from an African Doctor and His Hospital* is a page-turner that keeps readers engrossed in the stories. Read it with caution, though; the book is likely to inspire you to join the Faith Alive story yourself."

Philip R. Fischer, MD
Professor of Pediatrics at the Mayo Clinic

"Having met both Mother Teresa and Dr. Chris Isichei, I believe that the Lord has 'cut them from the same cloth.' Prepare to be challenged and inspired!"

Rev. Richard McDermott
Senior Pastor, First Presbyterian Church
Fort Collins, Colorado

"These are stories that need to be heard and Erika Wiebe Nossokoff gives voice to them. Few of us have the opportunity to sit with individuals who live in poverty and poor health and watch their eyes and facial expressions as they relate their very personal experiences. Many of the stories are troubling, but the people who tell them are always filled with hope. Erika honors the storytellers by allowing us to share in their experiences—experiences that will move us. We are enriched by having someone tell us firsthand about a Nigerian physician called Dr. Chris, a hospital called Faith Alive, and the people who are transformed by the good works of faithful Christians."

Arthur J. Ammann, MD
President of Global Strategies
for HIV Prevention

"These captivating, fast-paced stories about Nigerians are relevant to our lives around the world. Dr. Chris challenges us, by his inspiring example and urging, to energize our lives and our churches to serve with great impact. People go to Faith Alive in Nigeria to help but end up getting hope, new perspectives, and sometimes even new careers from their life-changing experiences."

T. Russell McCahan
Executive Director, Faith Alive USA, Inc.

"These fascinating stories prove that modern day miracles happen. Since I first visited the Faith Alive Hospital in 2009, I knew that everyone needed to hear how God is working through faithful servants there. This book shows how God uses Dr. Chris and the staff to create an oasis of hope in a country otherwise known for negative news."

Nkem Chukwumerije, MD, FACP
Physician Director, Utilization Management
Kaiser Foundation Hospital
Panorama City, California
President-Elect, Association of Nigerian
Physicians in the Americas (ANPA)
Board Member, Faith Alive USA, Inc.

"These heartfelt stories about Faith Alive Hospital's impact on Nigerians provide inspiration that can change our lives around the world. Whether or not you accept Dr. Isichei's invitation to travel to Nigeria—and I hope you do—reading this book will make a positive difference in your life."

Sally Barlow
Founder of Faith Alive Foundation-Nigeria's
Save-A-Life Program
and former U.S. Coordinator

"This is the story of Dr. Chris Isichei, his profoundly humble dedication to providing free health care to the less privileged in Jos, Nigeria, and his founding of Faith Alive Hospital and Counseling Center. It was not accomplished by him alone, but it could never have been accomplished without him—the founding father—daddy of the Faith Alive family. This book is for those of us who may have lost faith, rejected faith or found faith to be unnecessary in our lives. The facts recounted stimulate deeper consideration of faith, belief, unbelief, coincidence and mystery, and maybe the meaning of life."

Pamela Brown, RN, MPH
Epidemiologist, Health Services Bureau
New Mexico Corrections Department
Co-investigator with Dr. Isichei
on HIV Prevalence Study, 1998

"If you're like many Christians in much of the world today, we're comfortable, safe, and secure; we believe in Jesus but, in our most honest moments, confess that we wonder why we don't experience the Jesus in action that we read about in our Bibles. This book beautifully tells the stories of Christ-followers I was fortunate to come to know personally who know little of comfort, safety, or security but experience Jesus in action daily. They have found faith that is alive, hope that endures, and joy unending. We can learn a lot from their lives. Their stories inspire us to move outside of the comfort and safety in which we have hidden our faith and into the world around us—a world that is hurting, lonely, and afraid, a world desperately in need of the Jesus who lives in each of us who have found him as Savior and chosen to follow him as Lord. Mungode, Allah."

Biana M. Grogg, RN, BSN, SPHN
Public Health Nursing Director
Madera County Public Health Department
Madera, CA
Faith Alive Hospital Administrator
Jos, Nigeria, 2006 – 2009

"Authentic witness! Before the anti-virals, hundreds lived because of 'Living Faith' captured in Erika Nossokoff's page turning portrayal of Dr. Chris Isichei and the Faith Alive family in Nigeria that reminds us that Christ lives through love in action."

William A. Blattner, MD
Co-Founder, Institute of Human Virology
School of Medicine
University of Maryland

"Committed to providing free holistic health care to the poor, Dr. Chris confronts extraordinary challenges with extraordinary faith. With truthful detail, Erika engages you with each moving story as she makes the present situation meaningful by weaving events in the past. Hope for West Africa Foundation was formed to support this lifesaving work."

Diane Blattner
Co-Founder
Hope for West Africa Foundation

FAITH alive

ERIKA WIEBE NOSSOKOFF

FOREWORD BY DR. CHRISTIAN O. ISICHEI

FAITH alive

STORIES OF HOPE & HEALING FROM AN
AFRICAN DOCTOR & HIS HOSPITAL

TATE PUBLISHING
AND ENTERPRISES, LLC

Published by Tate Publishing & Enterprises, LLC
127 E. Trade Center Terrace | Mustang, Oklahoma 73064 USA
1.888.361.9473 | www.tatepublishing.com

Tate Publishing is committed to excellence in the publishing industry. The company reflects the philosophy established by the founders, based on Psalm 68:11,

"The Lord gave the word and great was the company of those who published it."

Book design copyright © 2013 by Tate Publishing, LLC. All rights reserved.
Cover design by Chris Harper
Interior design by Jomar Ouano
Author photo by Cathy Richardson

Published in the United States of America

ISBN: 978-1-62295-531-2
1. Religion / Christian Life / Inspirational
2. Religion / Christian Ministry / Missions
12.02.07

Dedication

For my Nigerian brothers and sisters in Christ who inspire me to choose hope. May our faithful God continue to shine in and through you.

Acknowledgements

Dr. Christian Isichei, a.k.a. Dr. Chris, challenges us to set seemingly impossible goals so that only God gets the glory. This book project qualifies for this first time author, so I must first and foremost thank God. He gave me the vision to give a broader voice to his faithful servants at the Faith Alive Hospital and the power to spend three years researching, writing, fact-checking, rewriting, and finally publishing this collection of dramatic, linked narratives.

Second, I pray that this book honors the Faith Alive vision planted by Dr. Chris for a self-sustaining, internationally recognized medical and social services center that meets the needs of humanity in a holistic way. He spent countless hours sharing information with me and editing each chapter for accuracy. May his compassion, humility, selfless service, and deep faith in Jesus Christ reap a harvest of blessings not only for his biological and Faith Alive families, but also for the Nigeria he calls home.

My gratitude goes to the entire Faith Alive family, both in Nigeria and partners around the world (some of whom are listed in a special section at the back of the book). I am especially grateful for those whose stories are part of this book, some of whom requested that I change their names in the book. They graciously let me probe into some of the darkest points of their lives so that others might see God's healing light. I pray that my retelling of their stories does not cause more pain, but rather reminds them of God's love and faithfulness.

This book would not be in print if my two writing groups—Broad Horizons and FPC—had not provided endless encouragement and editing. I also appreciate Paul Gossard and Susan Richardson for their freelance editing, as well as Chris Harper for the front cover design, Cathy Richardson, Craig Fitzgerald, and Ryan Day for the photographs, Ezekiel Emealereta Udubrae for the painting of Dr. Chris, and James Stockham for the graphic of Nigeria.

Last but definitely not least, I thank my family. My husband, Mark, has been my biggest supporter. He never once spoke a word of regret since that day in 2009 when I said that someone needed to write a book about Dr. Chris and the people at Faith Alive. He looked directly at me and said, "You." I also thank our daughter, Jenny, who paved the way by visiting Faith Alive first and giving me the courage to follow. God willing, soon our son, Austin, will also experience the journey.

Table of Contents

Now faith is confidence in what we hope for
and assurance about what we do not see.

Hebrews 11:1

Foreword

Dr. Christian Ogoegbunem Isichei, "Dr. Chris," 2012

God has been with me through all of life's ups and downs. Like the biblical Joseph, I have experienced God's faithfulness. In Nigeria, my senior brothers never threw me in a pit, but a group of men beat me, stripped me naked, tied my hands and feet, and left me for dead in the bush. I was never sold into slavery, but I was imprisoned by my fears of disease and death. A drought did not destroy my food, but extreme poverty plagues my country. Through it all, I have seen God redeem every doubt and suffering. I am alive today to testify that God is victorious and will never leave us.

God also brings the right people at the right time to be vision builders. Erika Wiebe Nossokoff is one of those people. God brought her to Jos, Nigeria for the first time in 2008 after her daughter Jennifer visited; Erika is now Faith Alive Foundation-Nigeria's International Coordinator who helps connect our vision with the world. Her passion for God's work and the people at the Faith Alive Hospital give us great encouragement. The staff knows her as "Erika from America," the optimistic, godly woman who is now part of our extended family. She is a hard worker and wonderful writer who, with the support of her devoted husband Mark, spent three years interviewing, writing, and rewriting these true stories.

This book represents me, the Faith Alive Hospital, and some of the many people whose lives I have been blessed with the opportunity to touch. I highly recommend this book, filled with infectious stories, to everyone who desires to leave a legacy by investing in our greatest asset: human lives.

As your read each story, I encourage you to think about God's faithfulness in your own life. If you are in a pit right now, God is with you. If you are on a mountain top, God is with you. He is faithful and has a plan for your life.

This foreword would not be complete without giving thanks to our heavenly Father for the support of my wonderful wife, Mercy, and our children, Emily, Prince, and Joseph. We give God all the glory.

May God bless each of you, now part of the worldwide Faith Alive family, with an extra measure of hope and healing as you read this book.

Your co-laborer in his vineyard,

Christian O. Isichei, MD
Founder and Coordinator
Faith Alive Foundation-Nigeria

Timeline

1990:   Dr. Chris poisoned.

1992:   Amos burned in fiery car accident.

1996:   Dr. Chris returns from study in Albuquerque,
        New Mexico, USA with $333 to start Faith
        Alive as a counseling center in a four-room flat
        at 6c Tafawa Balewa Street in Jos, Nigeria.

        Dr. Chris meets Dr. Mercy.

        Chioma forced into marriage.

1997:   Faith Alive expands services to 200 patients
        with the help of volunteer staff.

1998:   Faith Alive expands to a cluster of one-story
        buildings at the current 29 Zik Avenue campus.

        Kate comes to Faith Alive.

1999:   Dr. Chris marries Dr. Mercy, studies at Mayo
        Clinic in Rochester, Minnesota, USA.

2000: Kate leads HIV-positive support group, officially opens elementary school.

2001: Dr. Chris's life threatened by Christians.

Pastor Esther's husband dies.

2002: Pastor Esther's son dies.

Helen comes to Faith Alive for treatment.

2003: Pastor Esther comes to Faith Alive.

2004: Dr. Mercy travels to the American White House; PEPFAR medications arrive at Faith Alive to treat over 2,000 HIV-positive patients.

Chioma comes to Faith Alive after her husband dies.

Chede comes to Faith Alive.

2005: Ogbonna comes to Faith Alive.

2006: Single-story Faith Alive facility burns.

Three-story hospital construction completed and dedicated at Faith Alive's tenth anniversary celebration.

Little Chris born with heart defect.

2008: Pastor Esther leads "HIV and the Church" training.

Caroline's home burned during violent crisis in Jos.

Erika visits Faith Alive for the first time.

2009: Dr. Chris abducted.

2010: Little Chris receives heart surgery.

2011: Faith Alive celebrates fifteenth anniversary, treats more than 10,000 patients a year.

Dr. Chris begins mentoring program.

Pastor Esther remarries.

Nigeria, Africa

Introduction:
Journey to Jos

Do not be anxious about anything, but in everything, by prayer and petition, with thanksgiving, present your requests to God. And the peace of God, which transcends all understanding, will guard your hearts and your minds in Christ Jesus.

Philippians 4:6 & 7

January 2008

Meeting an incredible African doctor and his hospital staff changed my career, my calendar and my checkbook. Before I arrived in Nigeria for the first time, though, I only thought about what a man had said moments earlier. We had stood next to each other waiting to board a Nigerian-bound airplane, our pale faces singled out among a sea of African passengers.

I made eye contact with him and asked, "Where are you headed?"

"To Lagos for business. You?"

"To Jos," I answered, trying not to reveal that this was my first overseas flight. "To an amazing hospital that serves a lot of AIDS patients."

He wrinkled his forehead and shook his head from shoulder to shoulder. "Ohhh, I would never go to Jos. Much too violent."

Wait. He's going to Lagos, God, the city known for carjackings, kidnappings, and extortion of westerners, and he thinks that Jos is too dangerous? It took me years to get over my fear of going to Africa, let alone any place without reliable electricity and running water. What have I gotten myself into?

"But I'm with my team from church," I told the man, nodding toward the eleven others in an attempt to reassure myself more than this stranger.

"Hmmm," he said. "Good luck."

Luck? I'm counting on you, God, to protect me. You will keep me safe, right?

"You, too," I said before I turned away from him and back to my mission. My first small step onto the plane felt more like a gigantic leap of faith.

Once on the plane, I hoisted my carry-on bag, packed neatly with anti-malaria pills and a mini-pharmacy, into an overhead bin. The space underneath the seat in front of me barely had enough room for my purse, bulging with my Bible, crossword puzzles, and a traveler's insurance policy. The fine print included provisions, in the event of unfortunate circumstances, for a horizontal flight home in the airplane's lower section.

Sitting down and buckling my seatbelt, I realized that no amount of planning or prescriptions could save me from real or perceived threats. Only God could, and I needed him now more than ever.

Up in the air, I tried to force sleep, but my mind needed to revisit why I had agreed to this trip.

I thought back to being a thirteen-year-old when I had heard African missionaries speak passionately at my church. That evening, I had pulled my quilted comforter up to my chin while the blustery Kansas winds whipped against my bedroom windows. Though safe and warm, I could not quiet my thoughts. Visions of dark-skinned people sporting face paint and wielding spears flashed through my head as I tossed and turned.

Lord, I want to be faithful to you. But Africa seems so different, so distant, so dangerous. Please don't ever send me there.

I eventually fell asleep with my eyes and heart closed to world missions.

Thirty years later, I received a personal invitation to visit Africa. Russ McCahan, a man from our church where I worked as the director of equipping ministries, had gone to the Faith Alive Hospital in Jos and come home with nothing but contagious enthusiasm. All his conversations revolved around the hospital and its Nigerian founder, Dr. Christian Isichei, who started it with $333 and a vision to serve the poor.

"You're on the list to go next time," Russ told me.

Yeah, right, I thought. But my interest rose and defenses lessened each time I heard him talk about Faith Alive. I did not go on the next trip, but my twenty-two-year-old daughter, Jenny, jumped at the chance to enrich her medical studies. Russ assured me that the founder, affectionately known as Dr. Chris, only invited visitors when he felt that conditions were safe.

Please protect her, God, I prayed every day during her trip. She returned home without a scratch, echoing Russ's invitation.

"Mom," she said. "You have to go to Faith Alive. The people are amazing!" My lips formed a smile, but my eyes revealed doubt.

"You'll be okay, Mom. Really."

God, should I take her advice? If she went to Africa and came back alive, maybe I could, too. Besides, this could give us a new connection. And I'm ready to try something new. Is this your plan for the second half of my life?

From the comfort of my home in a Colorado college town that evening, I flipped open my laptop and Googled Nigeria. *Most populous African country. State: Plateau. City: Jos, home to more than one million people from Nigeria's three main tribes: Igbo, Hausa, and Yoruba. Jos, situated at an invisible yet palpable continental fault line dividing Muslims in North Africa from Christians in sub-Saharan Africa.*

I clicked around and read that in 2000, twelve northern Nigerian states enforced Sharia, a Muslim law that in its fundamental interpretations enforces strict punishment for a myriad of offenses, including women who do not cover their faces in public, homosexuals, and Muslims who abandon the faith. This law seemed to be one of the many long-term contentions between Muslims and Christians, as well as indigenous and non-indigenous people groups, that often incited bloodshed there. I quickly clicked on an African map to make sure that Nigeria was not near Rwanda where I had heard about genocide. I sighed with relief when I saw the distance.

Then I Googled the Faith Alive Hospital. *Medical and social services, all free of charge to over 10,000 patients. About 150 staff and volunteers prescribing hope and saving lives.*

God, this place looks inspiring. Maybe it's okay for me to go. But what would I do there? The only medical skills I have are adhering bandages and reading thermometers. Wouldn't it be better for me to send money instead of paying for my airfare? I need a clear sign if you want me to go on our church's next trip.

Within a few months, I learned that Faith Alive needed an American volunteer to lead their Save-A-Life personal sponsorship program that matched HIV-positive patients with sponsors who paid for lifesaving antiretroviral medications. With a rapidly increased heart rate, I sensed that this leadership opportunity might be a good match with my skills.

God, is this a sign from you? To do this role well, I really should go to Nigeria and meet some of the patients. But I'll need you to help me get over my fears.

I decided to give myself two weeks to pray and talk with friends and family about going to Africa. Based on my feelings each day, I would mark either "yes" or "no" on my color-coded calendar. People, especially my husband, encouraged me to go. My calendar two weeks later showed a "yes" on each day, so I signed up for the next trip.

After reminiscing and praying on that flight in 2008, I unbuckled my seatbelt and stepped off the airplane at Nnamdi Azikiwe International Airport in Abuja, Nigeria's capital. My eyes locked on numerous camouflage-clad men patrolling the airport with AK-47s hung over their shoulders. I tried to walk by them casually, mimicking the Nigerian travelers who seemed used to this display of power.

Okay, God, I'm totally surrendered to you. I have no control over anything except my responses.

I anxiously scanned the crowds for Dr. Chris. Just then I saw his smiling face as a uniformed official escorted him to greet our team in customs. He looked much like he had when I met him during one of his trips to the United States.

"Dr. Chris!" I said with a mix of excitement and relief.

"You are welcome," he said to us with the traditional Nigerian greeting. A sense of divine calm instantly flowed through me as I reached down to hug him.

After clearing customs, we pushed our tired bodies and heavy luggage through crowds of young men vying to carry our bags. We eventually loaded all our cargo into two Faith Alive vans.

"How long is the drive to Jos?" I asked.

"Three or four hours, God willing," Dr. Chris said. I later learned that the time depended on our drivers' speed and skill to navigate through heavy rains, roadside accidents, herds of slow-moving cattle, or armed robbery ambushes.

As we pulled away from the parking lot, I inhaled stifling diesel motorbike fumes saturated with smoke from cooking fires. Each breath took us farther away from pure, familiar Rocky Mountain air. I stared out the window at the roads lined with throngs of men, women, and children wearing brightly colored outfits. Women secured babies to their backs with extra fabric while walking barefooted, hips swaying and heads balancing fruit-filled baskets. Hundreds of people lined the streets, apparently waiting to cram into taxis. I noticed a few men wearing slacks, dress shirts, and ties while going into or coming out of a few modern hotels and restaurants.

"Look over there," Dr. Chris said, pointing to the National Ecumenical Christian Church in Abuja. I saw the high arches adorning the church's perimeter. He then aimed his arm in the opposite direction, toward a gold dome and four minarets jutting above the landscape. "That is the National Mosque on the other side of Independence Avenue."

What a contrast. The road between the mosque and church is a lot like that metaphorical fault line dividing Muslims and Christians in Africa. I hope there won't be any shaky movements between the two groups while we're here. I wonder what Dr. Chris thinks about Muslims?

As though he could read my mind, he said, "You will see that at Faith Alive, we treat everybody, whatever their faith. To me, Islam stands for, 'I shall love all Muslims.'"

We snaked our way out of Abuja on decently paved roads with sporadic traffic lights and street markings observed as suggestions. With each turn, I noticed that the roads became bumpier and the dry, brown landscape became more rural. Our driver slowed and swerved around numerous villages' speed bumps fashioned by logs and boulders. I was not sure whether to look at or ignore the children in tattered clothes who ran up to our van's windows, offering us live chickens, bread, palm oil, newspapers, or miniature green-and-white Nigerian flags.

Between villages, I saw clusters of mud huts with thatched roofs, schools seemingly in the middle of nowhere, and boys no older than eight using sticks to herd groups of dirty-white, bone-thin oxen. We occasionally passed rugged trucks overflowing with cattle, mattresses, or people piled so high that I thought one pothole or quick swerve would propel them onto the road.

As much as I did not want to miss anything, jetlag saturated my body. I dozed off a few times until the van slowed in heavier traffic.

I woke to hear Dr. Chris say, "We are in Jos. It stands for 'Jesus our Savior.'"

About an hour into the city, we finally stopped at the three-story hospital painted white with bright-blue trim, its tin awning above the entrance spread out like a cross. I saw the signpost in front that bore a photo of Dr. Chris, his surgeon wife, Dr. Mercy, and their three children. The caption read: "Faith Alive: Where God Himself Is At Work."

Because it was Sunday, the only staff there were for emergencies. Dr. Chris invited us to follow him under the metal awning and into the waiting room. My eyes had not yet adjusted to the darkness caused by frequent power outages, so I did not immediately see the hundred or so AIDS patients at their weekly support group meeting. With some afternoon light shining through the windows, I made out their shapes pressed against each other as they sat on wobbly, wooden benches. They stood to greet us, welcoming us with smiles and energetic greetings. Then, they sang vibrant praise songs that reverberated off the walls and into our hearts.

Lord, how can they be so happy when HIV streams through their blood and so little money flows through their hands? I expected to see miserable, desperate, dying people here.

During the next twelve days, we met extraordinary people who considered Drs. Chris and Mercy their loving parents. I saw Dr. Chris pull naira, Nigerian currency, from his wallet to give patients in need. Someone told me that he rarely said no to genuine requests, erring on the side of trust rather than suspicion, grace rather than judgment, and mercy rather than punishment.

Laughter erupted as Dr. Chris waddled through a prenatal class as if he, too, were carrying a baby. During a serious meeting, he must have sensed the staff's discouragement because he jumped to his feet and started dancing and singing. Soon everyone joined him, their lips and hearts turned upward.

I watched, over and over, as Dr. Chris immunized people against despair and prescribed hope. Counseling a depressed patient with tuberculosis, he touched the man's hand and said, "It is not so bad. You will soon be better." I asked Dr. Chris if he, or we, might catch the virus.

He said, "Our immune systems are strong. His is weak from AIDS." Still, I stayed away from the separate tuberculosis area and washed my hands often, even though the room was well ventilated.

The only thing I caught was their infectious joy. It filled my spirit in a way that rivaled my wedding day and the first time I held each of my newborn children. In all my years of ministry and community missions, I had never experienced God at work so powerfully in such seemingly dire situations.

Nearly two weeks after I first stepped on African soil, the day came for our return flight. I prayed as I boarded the airplane.

Lord, I want to take the Nigerians' hope home with me. Their faith is fully alive amidst pain, their joy is immense despite suffering, and their calmness is contrasted by seeming chaos. Please, I want a deep, lasting faith and joy like theirs. I don't want to be a missionary tourist whose spiritual journey ends when I'm back on American soil.

Our team returned home safely with the mission to continue our partnership with Faith Alive. With promptings and confirmations from that trip, one young woman enrolled in seminary, another in nursing school, and another eventually married a Nigerian pastor.

Because I said yes to God and went to Nigeria, the African AIDS epidemic became personal. "They" were no longer a statistic but became part of my extended family connected by cell phones and the Internet when available.

Their life stories changed the next chapter of my life. After my first trip to Jos, I resigned my paying church job to become our church's volunteer mission and outreach leader. I finished that fulfilling role three years later when I accepted the role as Faith Alive Foundation-Nigeria's U.S. Coordinator, recently expanded to International Coordinator. I now spend my time equipping others around the world to connect with the wonderful people at Faith Alive.

Allow me to give you a front-row seat to their heart-wrenching yet uplifting life stories recreated from actual events as told to me. While you do not need a visa or immunizations for this literary journey, you do need to be prepared. The conditions in Jos are extreme when viewed through a Western lens. In addition to religious and political tensions, the masses struggle to survive on less than $2 a day in this country rich with natural resources.

The harsh reality of their lives shows how people can endure and how God's faithfulness—through Dr. Chris and his team—transforms victims into victors. While their stories are unique to their context, we can relate to their needs for hope and healing.

May your heart be inspired and your faith in Jesus Christ increase as you read each chapter linked by Dr. Chris and our faithful God who is, as Nigerians say, "on ground" with us. Listen for what God might be saying to you. Who knows? Maybe he is inviting you to take an exciting leap of faith.

part
1

FAITH ALIVE
FOUNDING FAMILY

A faithful founder and his ministry: to
know one is to understand the other.

Christian, Mercy, Emily, Prince, and Joseph Isichei, 2010

My Name is Christian

A good name is more desirable than great riches.

Proverbs 22:1a

September 2001

Dr. Chris woke before the roosters with full confidence that the sun would emerge. In his meager Nigerian flat, he swept the floor, read his Bible, and reviewed some paperwork before sitting down for breakfast with his wife, Mercy.

"In Jesus' name," he bowed and began praying aloud.

"Amen," she said.

"Lord, we thank you for this food and the miracle of a new sunrise. However, whenever, and whatever you ask of us today, our answer in advance is yes. We ask for your protection for our family and Faith Alive. In Jesus' name we have prayed. Amen."

Careful not to spill the bowl of sugar-laden oatmeal that his wife had cooked on their gas stove, Dr. Chris ate. He got up and tucked his blue dress shirt into his trousers and smiled at their two-week-old daughter, Emily. His beard, which had not seen a razor for at least three busy weeks, brushed the top of her head as he leaned down to kiss her good-bye.

The screen door banged behind him as he walked toward his Jeep. He got in and drove to his salaried job at Jos University Teaching Hospital (JUTH) where he spent the morning and early afternoon instructing medical students. As soon as classes ended, he quickly drove across town to Faith Alive, the hospital that he founded five years earlier.

He parked in front of the hospital, got out of his Jeep, and darted through the entrance. "Good afternoon," he said to the dozen or so patients already waiting in the queue on backless wooden benches. They nodded and returned his greeting.

"How now?" he asked his fellow volunteers.

"Doctor," they said with respect usually reserved for someone twice his size. "We are fine."

Armed with a stethoscope, vitamins, and a Bible, Dr. Chris sat behind a weathered wooden desk in his office. He called in his first patient and took no notice of the routine Islamic call to prayer blaring from nearby loudspeakers through the room's paper-thin walls.

Before long, a disheveled young man rushed into the hospital. He uttered between panted breaths, "There is danger...near...the mosque...all hell is loose! I saw bodies...on the ground."

Recognizing the man as a friend's son and seeing blood on his shirt, Dr. Chris jumped up to help.

"Sit, sit down," Dr. Chris said, pointing to his own chair. "Let me check you. What happened?" Dr. Chris listened to the story of blood and chaos as he examined the young man's wounds. Soon, more people came into the hospital with similar injuries and panicked expressions. The staff offered triage and referred people with major injuries to better-equipped area hospitals.

Hours after the violence began, Dr. Chris treated his last patient of the day. His normally bustling city with more than a million residents seemed eerily dark and quiet except for humming generators. He switched on the hospital's small black and white television to watch the latest news.

"Jos sustained mass casualties today," the announcer said. "Witnesses describe Muslim youth beating a Christian woman whom they felt walked too close to a mosque during afternoon prayers. Outraged Christians nearby were seen retaliating with stones and sticks, exploding like gasoline sparked by matches. Already, before the day is over, hundreds of dead bodies lay strewn over the sloped landscape."

Lord, have mercy! I need to be near my wife and daughter.

The screen then flashed to the governor who assured listeners that the situation was now under control.

God, is it really safe for me to go home?

He walked cautiously out the door. Seeing nobody on the street, he decided to risk the drive home with his friend's son who had waited for a ride. They got into his Jeep. Dr. Chris started the ignition and sped as quickly as he could down streets devoid of normal bumper-to-bumper motorists honking horns and zigzagging around potholes, accidents, and stray goats.

As he slowed at a corner, Dr. Chris noticed shadowy figures racing over the hill toward them. Before he could step on the gas pedal, the mob of young men descended on his Jeep—but not before his friend's son somehow managed to open the passenger-side door and sprint to safety.

"Kill him!" the mob screamed at Dr. Chris. They waved bats, pipes, and axes. Two of them yanked his door open and pulled him from the Jeep.

He inhaled smoke invading the air and correctly assumed that it drifted from victimized businesses and homes. Ahead, he saw other attackers with machetes hacking a struggling victim.

"Are you a Christian or a Muslim?" shouted one of the tall hooligans. Dr. Chris guessed them to be between eighteen and twenty-five years old.

Oh Lord, what answer will save me? Are these Christians or Muslims? Give me courage to stand for you, dear God, dear God, dear God.

With a trembling voice, he declared what might be his last words.

"I am Christian."

The apparent ringleader stepped closer.

"Prove it," he slurred. "Because if you are a Muslim, you will die right here." Sour breath and spit spewed toward Dr. Chris's face. The fighter seemed bent on drawing blood.

Oh dear Lord, can this boy really be a Christian? Will he be able to control his rage?

Dr. Chris carefully chose his words.

"See, I know the Bible. Our Father, who art in heaven," he began, "hallowed be thy name. Thy kingdom come, thy will be done...." His pace accelerated as he recited a few of the hundreds of verses that were written in his memory and on his heart.

As sweat dripped from his temples and armpits, he wondered if the hoodlum could smell his fear.

Will I live to tell of this? Surely this attacker knows that most Muslims would not memorize all these Scriptures.

The other aggressors started to back off, but this hooligan's eyes glazed with hateful rage.

"You're lyin'!" yelled the thug, raising a club studded with dozens of nails. It stood poised to rip the innards out of any victim who had the bad luck to drive along this specific road on this particular evening.

Dr. Chris's eyes widened.

Please, God, reciting Scripture alone is not enough. Help!

"Pleeeeease—please let me show you my card," pleaded Dr. Chris as he carefully reached into his pocket. "I am Christian. Please let me go."

The boy took a long pause. He looked at the card. Through the thick, smoky air, he squinted to read: "Dr. Christian Isichei, Faith Alive Foundation."

"See," Dr. Chris said, "my name is Christian. No Muslim would have this name."

The boy threw the card back at Dr. Chris and said, "Get outta here. And stay away."

As the boy turned, Dr. Chris had already jumped into his Jeep and started speeding away.

Thank you, God almighty. Thank you, Baba and Mama. Only God would know that having this name would save my life at such a time as this. Thank you, Jesus, thank you, thank you. I am coming home to you, my dear Mercy and Emily. God willing, I am coming home safely.

He finished the Lord's prayer with a newfound appreciation for *lead us not into temptation and deliver us from evil. For thine is the kingdom, and the power, and the glory, forever and ever. Amen.*

Once safe at home, he embraced and clung to his wife. Together, they prayed for the drunken rebels who professed to be Christian but were caught in a wave of violent desperation.

Grant them grace and mercy, Father God. And forgive them, for they know not what they do. Show them a path of peace found only in you, whatever life's circumstances.

●　　●　　●

To this day, Dr. Chris continues to pray regularly for Nigerians—both Christians and Muslims—in this country he loves dearly. Faith Alive treats people of any belief, lined side-by-side at the hospital. He believes that all Nigerians need to seek God, live peacefully, and invest in their own country.

Dr. Chris also wants people to know and live into the meaning of their names.

"See," I once heard him tell one of his patients. He searched for a pen, wrote the word *Christian* on a torn piece of scrap paper, and covered the first six letters. Then he leaned forward, peered over his reading glasses, and said excitedly, "If you take away 'Christ' from my name, I am left with just the 'ian.' That stands for 'I Am Nothing' without him."

In crisis or in calm, Dr. Chris stays closely connected to Jesus. Through Christ, Dr. Chris is something, and somebody, who makes a difference for thousands of people.

What is true of Dr. Chris is also true of Faith Alive. In many ways, they are woven so tightly that they are indistinguishable. Without Christ working through Dr. Chris and protecting his life, the hospital would not exist. If he had been killed during that bloody crisis or the other times that people had tried to take his life, his patients might not be alive either. But like them, he is a survivor. And he wants the world to know that God is not just some distant deity in the sky. He is right here, on the ground, with us.

Birthday in the Bush

Be strong and courageous. Do not be afraid or terrified because of them, for the LORD your God goes with you; he will never leave you nor forsake you.

Deuteronomy 31:6

December 22, 2009

Faith Alive's cash flow problem troubled Dr. Chris. The hospital's bank account dwindled dangerously close to zero because its major donor's payment had not arrived.

God, you know that I need to pay something to more than 150 staff, even if some of them are volunteer. It is enough that they need their hard earned pay for necessary things like food and rent. But this month, to celebrate your son's birth, they also want to give their families small treats or new clothes. Please, help me give them what they have earned.

Taking precious time away from treating patients to provide for his staff, Dr. Chris straightened his tie over his crisply ironed shirt, put on his smartest jacket, and went to the bank. He knew that he needed to secure a loan before people traveled for the holiday. Instead of waiting the normal three days to process the loan, Dr. Chris spent all morning pleading with the bank employees to act immediately. He humbled himself before the manager, appealed to his compassion, and took personal responsibility for the loan.

His approach worked.

"Thank you," he gushed hours later as he shook hands with the manager. "Your labor of love will not be forgotten. God will surely reward you and your family." Dr. Chris then made sure to thank each banker personally before he left, giving them each sincere greetings and blessings.

Dr. Chris soon came out of the bank and got in the Toyota Prado with his driver, Goddy.

"Praise God!" he told Goddy. "God is so faithful. He has provided for us once again. Take me to Faith Alive, and then go home to start your holiday. I can drive myself home."

At Faith Alive, Dr. Chris passed the security guards and climbed the stairs to share the good news with the finance department. Then he checked with a few staff to see if they had any problems or needed help before driving himself home to rest with his children after school.

A little before 6:00 p.m., someone delivered a message to him from the on-call nurse.

"Doctor," the woman said. "We are sorry to bother you at home, but there is a seriously ill tuberculosis patient straining to breathe in our emergency room. He needs oxygen, but his family does not have money to go to a better-equipped hospital. What do you advise?"

Dr. Chris knew that other hospitals only treated patients who first paid at least some of their fee. Those hospitals also did not release patients until they paid the remaining fee. Dr. Chris treated emergency cases immediately and firmly believed in not charging fees—only accepting voluntary donations.

He needed to see this tuberculosis patient before deciding how to help. So he stepped carefully down his apartment's dilapidated entry step and surveyed the available vehicles locked behind his compound's gate. He looked past the clunky red van, air-conditioned bus and well-worn Jeep to the 4WD Toyota Prado displaying the PEPFAR (President's Emergency Plan for AIDS Relief) logo.

Only the Prado's tank held enough fuel to deliver him to and from Faith Alive. Even though his country was rich in oil fields, he knew it would be difficult if not impossible to get fuel in the evening because of the current fuel crisis. So he unlocked the Prado, got in the driver's seat, and drove about fourteen kilometers to the hospital.

After assessing the patient's physical symptoms and financial situation, Dr. Chris said to the nurse, "No other hospital will accept him. We have no choice but to keep him here. Please keep him comfortable, and help him as best you can."

Then, wanting to be done with this trying day, he decided to return home. But first he wanted to stop at the market to buy a special meal for his birthday the next day. He could almost taste the spicy, peanut-flavored suya kabob.

He opened his wallet to check his cash. Like the bank account that morning, there was not enough. He had to borrow money for the second time that day. This time, he only needed about N2,000, equivalent to $14. Musa, one of the ward attendants, provided the loan.

Dr. Chris climbed back in the Prado, set his neck on the low headrest, and took a deep breath before turning on the headlight.

Thank you, God, that soon I can enjoy the rest of the evening with my family and put this day behind me.

Once at the bustling outdoor market, he parked and started working his way through the shoulder-to-shoulder crowd. The smell of chicken and corn cooking over open fires increased his appetite.

Suddenly, three men surrounded him. They inconspicuously flashed their guns so that only Dr. Chris could acknowledge their power. He did not dare run.

The leader demanded in a low yet firm voice, "Do not make a scene or a lot of innocent people here will die."

They escorted him back to the Prado and demanded his keys. Once inside, they sandwiched him between two of them in the front seat and sped away.

"Give us all your money," the leader demanded.

Dr. Chris obediently gave them his meager birthday celebration money. They spit at him, insisting that he had more to offer.

"Give us your ATM card!" they ordered.

He did not have one. Nor did he own a cell phone, preferring to live unbound by phones' frustrating performance in Nigeria. He only carried one of his wife's cell phones when she traveled so they could check in with each other daily.

"You are lying!" they screamed. "We saw you at the bank this morning thanking people."

They pushed Dr. Chris down, forcing him to lie hidden on the car floor. His small body bounced as they passed over rough roads. They sped around a log speed-bump at a security checkpoint. Vehicles were supposed to stop and let police, armed with AK-47s, check for any violations like carrying weapons or too many passengers. But the driver forged ahead.

Oh, Lord, protect me from gunshots if the police open fire on us.

When nothing happened, he wondered why the Prado was not being stopped.

Are some of the police in on this?

His heart beat faster, and his stomach twisted at the thought.

His mind flashed back to a police checkpoint years earlier in neighboring Cameroon. Officials had stopped him at a mandatory roadblock.

"Brown envelope!" they had insisted, meaning that there should be bribe money in a brown envelope in the car's glove compartment.

Dr. Chris refused to ever pay a bribe, believing if he paid even once, word would spread, and he would always be expected to pay off any corrupt officials. He had ended up in a dank, crowded prison cell overnight before the authorities released him. The Cameroon government later sent him a letter of apology after a Nigerian official protested on Dr. Chris's behalf. But he remembered their cruel treatment.

That memory paled in comparison to this present fear.

The gunmen now spoke to each other in Ibo, Dr. Chris's tribal language. He heard them argue about what to do next.

"We have to kill him," one of the gunmen said.

"Yes," another agreed. "He is of no use to us, and he has seen our faces."

As the two began to plot, the youngest one said, "Maybe it is enough to take him to the bush and leave him there."

Oh, please God, give power to that one's voice.

Dr. Chris called on God to redeem his middle name, Ogoegbunem, meaning "my kindness will not kill me." He had acted kindly to his employees by ensuring their pay. Many employers would not have gone to such measures.

Please, God, do not let my kindness destroy me. I should never have gone to the bank today in one of our Faith Alive vehicles. I was so easily targeted. Ay, Lord, will this be my last day on this earth? Thank you that I blessed my family this morning.

Instead of their regular morning family devotions, he had left home early to get to the bank. He had decided to bless his wife and children quickly.

"Sweetheart, may God bless you and keep you for the day. Emily, Prince, and Joseph, may God guide you through the day."

Father God, please protect my family after they kill me.

After what seemed like hours but was probably about one, the ride became slower and bumpier. He heard branches swishing against the side of their vehicle and realized that they were approaching what would either be his grave or his place of release. The vehicle stopped. They pulled him out, pistol-whipped his neck, kicked him to the ground, and demanded that he take off all his clothes. He complied. They covered his head with a sack. He felt pressure as they tied something around the sack. He gasped for breath.

Keep me calm, help me breathe, he said silently both to himself and to God.

With his head covered, he struggled to hear what the men said.

Shivering and rationing his breaths, he felt a hand on his arm, directing him to walk. The two walked a few steps before Dr. Chris heard the nearby voice tell him to keep moving. Dr. Chris recognized the sound of this man's intonation. A sense of hope radiated through Dr. Chris's body. This was the gunman who wanted to spare Dr. Chris's life!

"Thank you," was all Dr. Chris managed to say through the sack when they stopped. He wished he had enough breath to add, "God bless you for sparing my life. God will surely reward you."

The abductor bound Dr. Chris's legs, tied his hands behind his back, and abandoned him in the dark bush.

Father God, thank you. Now please save me. Unbind me, Lord Jesus, and keep me alive for my family, for Faith Alive.

After a few minutes, he heard the Prado's engine roar—first loud and then growing fainter. He knew that he was by himself but not alone. God was with him.

He struggled to free himself and within minutes managed to loosen the bonds on his hands. Then he freed his face and his feet.

Thank you, Abba Father. Breathe in, breathe out, think, think, think. Guide my steps. Help me to see a way out of this darkness.

He blinked to adjust his sight to the cloudy night. He made out a faint light in the distance and instinctively walked toward it. Nearing a road, he crouched down to hide his nakedness. He waved for people in passing cars to stop, but they only stared at him like he was a possessed lunatic. They sped by.

He decided to walk down the street and hoped he would meet a sympathizer. Ahead, he saw a man's lit cigarette glowing in the dark. Dr. Chris moved toward him and begged.

"Please, I am not crazy. I have been robbed. They have taken my car, my money, and my clothes. Please!"

The man looked closely at Dr. Chris, who covered his private parts but revealed the truth.

"Here, take my jacket," the man said.

"Nagode. Nagode. Nagode," Dr. Chris gushed his thanks.

Together, they walked toward the light that shone from a small airport at Heipang near a police station. The police gave Dr. Chris a pair of trousers and listened to him recount the evening's nightmarish events. When they retraced the crime scene, they saw Dr. Chris's shirt and pants strewn about. He realized then that the abductors had bound his face with his own clothing.

"I must let my wife know that I am okay," Dr. Chris said. None of the policemen had much credit on their cell phones or fuel in their vehicles. He begged them to at least "flash" her—call her number and hang up after one ring, indicating for her to call that number back on her phone's credit instead. They agreed.

His wife and children were at home saying their nightly prayers together. Because Dr. Chris often came home late when he helped people, they had not been overly concerned. Their evening devotion focused on the book of Isaiah foretelling of Jesus Christ and his covenant with God to carry our sins, release us from darkness, and lead our paths.

Mercy heard the phone ring once and checked the number. Even though she did not recognize it, something prompted her to return the call in case of an emergency. Like her husband, people knew that she helped people at all hours. Maybe someone needed her.

"Hallo? Hallo? Who is this?" she asked before she heard her husband's voice tell her briefly about the night's fateful events.

"I am fine now," he reassured her.

"Thank God," she said. "He is faithful. Tonight the children and I studied how God directs our way and keeps us safe. He heard our prayers and guided your steps."

Not until 3:00 a.m. on his birthday did he return home to his family's warm embrace and praises of gratitude for God's faithfulness.

A few weeks later, Dr. Chris learned that the abductors were arrested in the neighboring country of Cameroon. They had tried to sell the Prado, but potential buyers were suspicious of the PEPFAR logo and papers they found belonging to Goddy and Faith Alive.

One gunman had escaped. Dr. Chris was not surprised to learn that it was the one who had spared his life.

Some months later, Dr. Chris traveled to Cameroon on an errand to retrieve the PEPFAR vehicle. While there, he met with the two robbers, forgave them, and prayed with them.

●   ●   ●

Reflecting on the night of his abduction, Dr. Chris told me that what he experienced paled in comparison to what our Lord Jesus endured.

"There is evil in this world," he said, "but with Jesus Christ, we are overcomers."

Yes, I thought, only with Jesus Christ. The savior whose birth I celebrated that holiday season also endured and overcame pain and persecution. He trusted God's redemptive, victorious plan.

Dr. Chris trusts God's plan. Since 2009, Dr. Chris celebrates his birthday, and the Lord's, with a newfound appreciation. He knows that each year of life on Earth is a gift of time to serve our faithful God, a lesson he remembers well from another horrific incident.

Coke Can

...we take captive every thought to make it obedient to Christ.

2 Corinthians 10:5b

1990 — Six years before founding Faith Alive

Dr. Chris finished examining a patient as part of his job at the university clinic. He wrote a prescription and heard a tap on the wooden door. Looking up, he saw one of his colleague's faces poking into the room, a commonly accepted interruption.

"Doctor," the colleague said. "I am sorry, but I need to leave. Do you need help at the bank today?"

"No, thank you," Dr. Chris said. "I went this morning and got the money. I am prepared to buy the car."

"Wonderful," the colleague said before closing the door and leaving.

Dr. Chris looked at his patient sitting in the white plastic chair and asked, "Is there anything else I can do for you? Are you satisfied?"

"I am satisfied," the patient said.

"Good. Would you call for the next patient?"

"Yes, Doctor," the patient said as he got up to leave. He took his prescription…and a new idea.

The day progressed normally for Dr. Chris as he treated a string of patients. Around 6:00 p.m., he finished some paperwork. Thirty-two years old and single, he did not need to hurry home to greet a wife and children.

He looked up when he heard a knock at his office door and said, "Yes? Enter."

He recognized the patient from earlier that day. Instead of a smile, the patient wore a pained expression.

"Doctor," the patient said quickly in Dr. Chris's native dialect. "Please, kind doctor, I need your help."

"What is the problem?"

"It is not me," the patient said, avoiding direct eye contact. "It is my friend Ikenna. I fear he might die with nobody to help."

"Where is your friend?"

"I will show you. Please, is there a way that you can come with me?"

Knowing that no other patients needed him at that moment, Dr. Chris jumped up and said, "I can."

"But I do not have transport," the patient said. "I rode a taxi here. Do you have a car?"

"Yes, yes, come with me," Dr. Chris said.

He grabbed his keys and medical bag before walking briskly toward his blue Volkswagen. The two got in, and Dr. Chris sped away, following the man's instructions to turn right here and veer left there as he snaked his car through Jos.

Dr. Chris soon noticed that fewer houses dotted the landscape as they entered the Dutse Uku neighborhood, considered an unsafe part of the city. But his compassion overrode any sense of hesitation.

"Here, it is right here," said the patient, pointing to a rundown home. "We must hurry."

Dr. Chris parked the car next to the house and reached for his medical bag. Then he jumped out of the car and followed the patient into the house, toward the screaming man.

Inside, Dr. Chris saw a handful of people standing around a man sprawled on the floor, wailing as if a ton of bricks had smashed him.

"Please help Ikenna," the patient said.

Dr. Chris bent down and said to Ikenna, "I am a doctor. What is the problem?"

"Ayi," Ikenna cried. "Yiiiii, my legs will not move. AYI," he struggled to say between gasps.

Dr. Chris checked Ikenna's vital signs. Temperature: normal. Pulse: slightly elevated. No bleeding. But the pain. That needed to be treated. Fortunately, Dr. Chris carried varying strengths of pain medication. He reached in his bag for the strongest.

"Does someone have a drink?" Dr. Chris asked.

A young woman quickly handed him a soda. Dr. Chris carefully propped Ikenna's back on an upholstered chair, upright enough for him to swallow the medicine.

Dr. Chris felt the man's legs, trying to pinpoint the pain's location. Ikenna showed by his closed eyes and clenched fists that all parts of his legs hurt.

"Let us wait and see what happens," Dr. Chris said. "This medicine should help."

Within a few minutes, Ikenna's cries turned into whimpers. Then, his breathing slowed to normal.

"Let us see if you can stand," Dr. Chris said to Ikenna, turning to the younger men for help. Two men reached down to steady his arms as Dr. Chris guided Ikenna to stand. Wobbly at first, he gradually rose and put pressure on his feet.

"Oh!" Ikenna said as if he experienced a miracle. "God is helping me to stand!"

Amazed at the speed and depth of recovery, Dr. Chris motioned for Ikenna to take a few steps.

Ikenna walked forward, first with his friends' help and then by himself.

"He is healed! Praise God!" the group shouted. "Oh, Doctor, we are so grateful. We must celebrate!"

Spurred by their enthusiasm, Dr. Chris grinned and said, "Yes, praise God!"

Wow, Father God. I do not understand it, but thank you for healing this man! If only every patient were this easy to treat.

The patient who had summoned Dr. Chris asked his fee for this successful medical treatment.

"I do not charge a fee," Dr. Chris said. "I give all thanks to God. You owe me nothing."

"Nothing?" the patient asked. "Please, at least recline and enjoy a Coca-Cola."

"Okay. Gladly."

The patient handed Dr. Chris an opened bottle of Coca-Cola and started to join the others in singing God's praises. As they clapped to the beat, Dr. Chris began to feel the room spinning like a wheel, first slow and then faster.

And then…darkness.

Nothing.

Oh, God…where am I? Where is everybody else? What happened?

With a sour taste in his mouth, he glanced at his blurry watch and realized that three hours had passed. His first few attempts to stand landed him back on the ground. Finally, he righted himself and wiped the dirt off his face. He recognized Ikenna's yard, now abandoned. And the Coca-Cola bottle.

Oh no, they drugged me.

Sensing danger, he turned toward the place he had parked his car. Only a dirt patch and emptiness filled the space.

God, where is my car? My car…and all the money I hid under the driver's seat to buy a more reliable car tomorrow! Oh, Lord, you know how hard I worked for that money. What will I do?

Then he willed himself to remember what his patient did not steal.

Thank you, God, that the drug did not kill me. Thank you for saving me.

He looked around for some means of help. Only a few cars passed, but he did not feel safe enough right then to trust a stranger.

Lord, who will help me?

Soon, he recognized a car driven by his insurance agent. Dr. Chris waved his arms and hobbled into the street.

"Please," he shouted, hoping the agent would recognize him. "Please help me—my car has been stolen."

The agent stopped and opened his car door for Dr. Chris to get in. He then recounted the night's events to the agent as they went to the police station. After reporting the theft and poisoning, Dr. Chris's agent took him home. There he decided to call an army officer friend to ask for help.

The next day, Dr. Chris's officer friend located the car but not the money.

Shaken by the drugging and robbery, Dr. Chris bought a bottle opener, put it on his keychain, and carried it with him to open his own drinks. He vowed not to drive his own car to visit patients, preferring to ride with others. But these precautions did not quickly or completely ease his mind.

His shaken sense of security provoked him to write his will and endure many sleepless nights. He worried about every ache and pain.

Oh, Lord, is there still poison in my body? Will I soon die?

He had no peace until he read the book *Pulling Down Strongholds* by John Osteen. It quoted 2 Corinthians 10:5 that says to cast down negative thoughts, making them obedient to Christ. The author reminded him that the devil works in our minds and imaginations. Like Job in the Bible, his circumstances alone did not overcome him—his thoughts did.

If my fears of imminent death are real, God, please let me die soon. If I am still alive on January 1, it will be a sign that I am healthy and cannot trust my doubts.

On January 1, 1991, Dr. Chris woke to cast down his strongholds and move forward.

●　　●　　●

Dr. Chris recognizes that many of his patients carry the poisonous burdens of fear, desperation, and depression. He relies on the meaning of his name Isichei—my thinking will uphold me—to counsel others.

I have heard him question newly diagnosed HIV-positive patients.

"How many people are in this room?"

Sometimes there are two, but more likely there are numerous people in the crowded examining rooms. Thinking this a strange question and possibly even a trick, patients give a sheepish but correct answer.

"Excellent!" he says.

Then he leans in close to them.

"Now, which one of us is going to die first?"

There is a long and awkward silence. Some look away to think. Others smirk a bit, perhaps thinking the question ludicrous.

They usually respond, "I don't know."

"Maybe it will be me," he says. "Maybe I will walk out of this hospital into the street and get hit by a speeding car. Or maybe one of us will not wake up tomorrow morning. Is there anyone, anywhere on earth, who woke up healthy this morning but will not be alive this evening?"

"Yes," they answer.

"Correct! Now, can you name any disease that used to have no cure, but today has a cure or at least is treatable?"

Unless they are in the medical field, they usually need a while to think. If they cannot think of a disease, he tells them about malaria, tuberculosis, or diabetes.

"Many people live healthy lives with HIV if they take their medicine," he tells them. "Tomorrow there may be a cure for HIV. We do not know. So just because you have HIV does not mean that you are the next one to die. Those who are sick will die. Those who are well will die. None of us can tell when he or she will die."

Then he peers over his lopsided reading glasses and annunciates slowly and emphatically.

"So…go…live…your…life. If God gives you one day, live it for him. If he gives you 100 years, live them for him."

Dr. Chris prescribes this kind of hope freely to his patients. It is not a Pollyanna, unrealistic notion that there is only good in the world. Positive thinking alone is not enough. His hope springs from something deeper. He cannot help but acknowledge the suffering around him. But he is confident that God can and will redeem it.

It was his conviction—his living faith—that led him to endure trials while waiting for a wife with similar beliefs.

Godly Woman

The LORD God said, 'It is not good for the man to be alone. I will make a helper suitable for him.'

Genesis 2:18

Mid-1990s

"Mr. Nine P.M."

If anybody knocked on Dr. Chris's door, his neighbors told visitors to come back at 9:00 p.m. He rarely missed the start of the daily news broadcasts, at least when the electric company provided power, even if he had to go back later in the night to his job at JUTH. If visitors' requests seemed urgent, he did not mind the interruptions.

Dr. Chris felt that getting home early wasted precious hours in which he could be helping people. Besides, spending a lot of time at home reminded him of his age—approaching forty and not yet married—a fact that brought his older sisters to their knees.

"God," they prayed with him, "please bless our junior brother with the joy of a godly wife and children. It is not good for a man to be alone."

He sensed worry in their voices that he might never marry, a concern he tried not to share. His sisters took responsibility for him after their parents died in the mid-1980s from medical complications. Sure, his sisters showed pride about his career accomplishments, but they did not want him to miss the satisfaction of being a husband and father with children to carry on his lineage and legacy.

His oldest sister, Grace, had started preparing him as a teenager to be a godly husband. She gave him a book, *On Becoming a Man,* to help him navigate hormones and associated temptations. Dr. Chris read and took seriously the author's advice to ask God for help controlling his natural desires. With God's help, he saved his body and heart for his future wife.

He once dated a woman until he realized their incompatibility. During a meal together, Dr. Chris learned about an ill person who needed immediate assistance. Leaving his half-eaten meal, he quickly left to offer help. His date did not hide her resentment and anger.

God, please show me a supportive woman, a merciful woman, who shares my values of working hard and investing in human lives—especially in emergencies. I will wait for the wife you have chosen for me.

Dr. Chris continued to work long hours, catching sleep when he found time between his job and offering free care to people who randomly showed up at his door. Oftentimes, he thought his flat looked like a triage unit for people with physical and emotional needs. Word had spread about his availability, but only patients came to his house—not a potential wife.

As part of his job at JUTH in mid-1996, he supervised projects funded by medical grants at a series of HIV-related workshops. During the first one, in Jos, the supervisory panel debated the validity of another doctor's submitted research methods.

"Where are your samples?" the panel's chairman asked the accused doctor directly.

The doctor stood up and answered. "Sir, I did not bring them this time. But you will see in my report everything that you need to know."

"If we do not see the samples, then how do we know that your findings are true? We cannot grant you funds if you fabricated these results."

Turning to the rest of his panel, the chairman said, "This is serious. How do we know that he even really collected the HIV results from children?"

Dr. Chris noticed a woman physician watching the interrogation intently.

During the next break, Dr. Chris saw her approach a member of the panel. He overheard her conversation.

"Sir," she said, "my name is Dr. Mercy Wakili from Maiduguri in Borno State."

"You are welcome," the panel member said. "Yes, I have heard of you and know that you are doing great work with HIV."

"Thank you. Regarding this doctor in question, I cannot speak for his samples or results…but I think that he deserves to be considered."

Dr. Chris stared at this bold doctor.

"I have met him before," she continued. "He had invited me to witness his study of street children because of my interest in helping young people with HIV. I was not able to go. But I do not think that a dishonest person would openly invite others to see what he is doing."

"Go on," the chairman said.

"That is all, sir," Dr. Mercy said. "I just ask that you give him a chance."

Wow, Lord, this is a woman who is not afraid to speak her truth, to defend someone whom everyone else in the room deems guilty.

Dr. Chris looked more closely at Dr. Mercy and saw more than a doctor. He eyed a beautiful woman without a wedding ring who wore a round, darkened birthmark between her eyebrows like a discernment radar. He witnessed the truth of her first name, Mercy, but would not know until later that *Wakili* means "wardhead," or one who acts as the village adviser or spokesperson.

Dr. Chris made a mental note to seek her out. Later that day, he made sure to introduce himself and start a friendship.

He attended the next workshop, located in Dr. Mercy's home city of Maiduguri in northern Nigeria with a high Muslim population. Because the workshop fell during the Islamic Ramadan season when Muslims fasted during daylight hours, the workshop organizers did not serve food. Dr. Chris appreciated that Dr. Mercy prepared and brought food for some of the

Christian participants, including Marc Bulterys from the United States.

During one of the group meals, she told them that she often cooked for many—even hosted those who needed a place to sleep. She said it seemed natural to open her home to whomever needed help. When she was about four years old, she discovered that all the other children living with her family did so because they needed a place to stay, not because they were related. She said she did not have siblings until her nine junior brothers and sisters were born.

Dr. Chris enjoyed Dr. Mercy's stories told during meals of traditional fried rice, chicken, and egusi soup made with melons and vegetables.

I could get used to this, he thought, affirming that one way to a man's heart is through a woman's cooking. With a satisfied stomach, Dr. Chris relaxed and the two began joking.

"Delicious!" he said. "Maybe I should take you to the United States the next time I go so you can cook Nigerian food for me!"

Quick to respond, Dr. Mercy said, "I will gladly go if you can fit me in your suitcase." Then she qualified her response. "But…I think you should take your wife instead."

"I do not have a wife—yet," he said. He dared not say what he hoped, that someday she would be the one to wear his ring, travel with him, and share his ministry.

They continued their friendship. Talking during workshop breaks in person and on their landline phones between workshops, Dr. Chris learned more.

She trailed him in age by nine years. Her father, a school headmaster by profession, also preached and started churches. Her mother, a homemaker, worked their farmland and later took a job in medical records. Their farm and her parents' marriage both prospered until her father did what was culturally acceptable at the time for Nigerian Christians. He added a junior wife—and then five more children—to the family during Dr. Mercy's secondary school years.

She also told Dr. Chris that she grew up in a primitive village where many people, though not her family, wore leaves like Adam and Eve. When the Nigerian government instituted their version of a "no shirt, no shoes, no service" policy at the markets, her father helped educate the village about wearing clothes. He also successfully convinced the villagers to discontinue a generations-old custom of killing the seventh newborn in each family.

"Why would they do such a thing?" Dr. Chris asked.

"I do not know," she said. "It was a traditional belief of theirs. Maybe at one time a seventh child did something terrible."

Dr. Chris's interest in this insightful and educated woman increased as time went on. She explained that her father highly valued curiosity. One cloudless night under the ceiling of stars, she said that her father looked up and asked her to imagine God and where he was. Her father's prompting to serve God encouraged her to study medicine and surgery, eventually focusing on general surgery.

Her reputation for freely feeding, hosting, and caring for people began during her university years. Some physicians and medical students expressed anger, saying that she stole their potentially paying patients. But that did not stop her. At times, there were so many people on the floor in her room that she had them sleep head to toe, toe to head, fitting them together like puzzle pieces.

Lord, is this woman real? Thank you for showing me someone beautiful who shares my values and lifestyle.

He also learned that in her final year at the university, she joined SWAN, the Society for Women and AIDS in Nigeria that educated prostitutes about HIV and provided condoms. Dr. Mercy visited their places of business, like warehouses with rooms attached by long hallways.

She told Dr. Chris about the time she had sat talking with the prostitutes when one of their clients arrived. Dr. Mercy had waited. The woman earned her money and then came back to finish her conversation with Dr. Mercy. Knowing that the women needed to earn money, Dr. Mercy said that she encouraged the prostitutes to learn different trades like styling hair or sewing clothes.

Hearing all this, Dr. Chris knew that she was "the one." After praying for and sensing God's confirmation, the decision came easily. He would ask her to marry him. The harder part would be getting her to agree.

Without much experience at asking a woman for a date, much less to marry him, he chose to write his intentions. His letter said, "I am a busy man and do not have time to date. I want to marry you because God told me that you are the one." No wine or roses—only the plain, simple truth.

Dr. Mercy would later tell him her thoughts. She had received the letter but did not think he was serious. A typical Nigerian man, she had thought, to be so bold. She set aside the letter and decided to slow the pace of their relationship.

A few months later, she happened to pick up a stack of papers and saw the letter again. He is a nice man, she thought, realizing that she should politely respond. She dialed his phone number.

"Hallo, Dr. Chris," she said, "this is Dr. Mercy."

"Hallo, hallo!" he said loudly into the phone.

"Thank you for the letter."

"Ah yes, so you received it?" he asked.

"Yes, I did…and I think that we should remain friends for now and get to know each other more."

Trying not to let his excitement show, he said, "Okay, okay. That would be good." She did not say "yes," but she did not say "no" either. And he noted that she had inadvertently called him on Valentine's Day, 1997.

Not until that summer when she came to Faith Alive's one-year anniversary did she seem to consider Dr. Chris's proposal seriously. Looking at the four-room office and hearing volunteers and patients speak so highly about his deep faith and compassion, she started to envision being his wife and joining him in this ministry.

He sensed a change in her heart and made excuses to visit her parents in Maiduguri. Dr. Mercy's mother welcomed him enthusiastically. He learned later that she told her daughter that Dr. Chris was definitely the one. A few other suitors over the years had proposed to Dr. Mercy, but none of them had impressed both Dr. Mercy and her mother.

Dr. Chris returned to his family and told them about his future bride. Perhaps worried that their unmarried adult brother might change his mind, his sisters rushed to Maiduguri to meet Dr. Mercy's family. His sisters said that they took one look at her with her family and felt convinced that God had finally answered their prayers.

With both families' required blessings, Dr. Mercy had one reservation.

"Chris," she said, now removing the formal title of doctor, "I need to tell you something."

"What, my dear?" he asked apprehensively.

"When we met, I was recovering from fibroid surgery."

Familiar with the procedure, he said, "Go on."

"And…and I do not know if I will ever be able to bear children."

He looked into her eyes. Without hesitation, he said, "My dear, if God wants us to have children, he will give them to us. If not, then he will not. It is okay."

He heard her sigh and saw her smile.

"Then my answer is yes," she told him.

On October 30, 1999, three years after they met, Dr. Mercy Wakili changed her surname to Isichei. They covenanted before God and hundreds of family and friends to love each other for better or worse, for richer or poorer, in sickness or health, as long as they both shall live. During the hours-long ceremony, they celebrated with singing, dancing, and thanking God for his faithfulness.

The married couple kept their honeymoon short because Dr. Chris needed to go back to the United States. They had both applied for visas to Rochester, Minnesota, where the new groom had received a six-month fellowship at the Mayo Clinic. Unfortunately, only his visa went through. He assured his bride that someday God would make a way for her to go to America. They decided that she would assume leadership at Faith Alive during his absence and agreed to stay connected by telephone.

"Hallo," Dr. Mercy said on the phone one afternoon after Dr. Chris arrived in Minnesota. "How are you?"

"Oh, hallo my dear," he said from underneath layers of blankets. He had experienced cold weather another year when he had studied in Albuquerque, but nothing like this frigid Minnesota winter. "I am fine, fine. But it is terribly cold here. How are you?"

"Fine, but I miss you," she said. "It is two o'clock in the afternoon here. What time is it there?"

"It is nine in the evening," he said. "I am just starting to watch the evening news. But you are a welcome interruption."

●　　●　　●

He now had a good reason, other than sleep and televised news, to come home each night. By August, 2001, the couple had news of their own—the birth of their daughter, Emily, followed later by their sons,

Prince and Joseph. The children have told me that they want to be either pastors or doctors, which does not surprise me given their upbringing.

Daddy's Legacies

Fix these words of mine in your hearts and minds; tie them as symbols on your hands and bind them on your foreheads. Teach them to your children, talking about them when you sit at home and when you walk along the road, when you lie down and when you get up.

Deuteronomy 11:18 & 19

August 2011

Dr. Chris drove his children to Abuja for a few days' vacation with cousins while his wife stayed in Jos to work. On the way, ten-year-old Emily finished telling a story. The bad monkey died, but the good monkey lived happily-ever-after.

"Excellent!" Dr. Chris told her. He turned to eight-year-old Prince, who sat in the front passenger seat, and said, "Prince, it is your turn now."

"But, Daddy," five-year-old Joseph interrupted from the backseat. "I want to tell a story!"

"You will tell one after Prince is finished," Dr. Chris said, "and then you can be the first to say a Bible verse."

After both boys told their stories, similar to Emily's but with different animals, Joseph recited a Bible verse.

Clamoring over his sister's voice, Prince recited the next verse, followed by Emily who recited two and then said, "Let us sing!"

"Very good," Dr. Chris said. "Emy, you start."

The children took turns choosing familiar songs, continuing even as their daddy slowed down for routine military checkpoints. The children finally dozed off about two-and-a-half hours into the ride, Emily's head on the back door, Joseph's body across Emily's lap, and Prince's chin drooped onto his chest.

● ● ●

During one of my visits to Nigeria, I enjoyed a delicious meal at the Isichei home. Dr. Chris asked Prince to pray before the meal. He offered a prayer to rival any adult's. His little brother Joseph started to cry.

Dr. Chris looked at his junior son and said, "I know you wanted to be the one to pray. You can pray for them before they leave."

When it came time to leave their home that evening, Joseph, now dressed in Spiderman pajamas, climbed onto his daddy's lap. We all bowed our heads. Joseph's prayer was not as clear as his brother's, but we understood the meaning.

I have also heard the other Isichei children pray in front of people. At Faith Alive, the staff customarily prays for visitors before they leave, so it did not surprise me when Dr. Chris called me up front during a staff meeting in 2011. Instead of him asking which of his staff would pray for me, he invited eight-year-old Prince.

"My son asked to say a prayer for Erika. He got up very early this morning to come with me."

Prince rose from his seat in the front row and stood next to me, not quite as high as my shoulders. I noticed his crisp, white shirt under his dark, black suit, all three buttons fastened. He stepped forward, took the microphone, and started to pray—for me, my family, and my safe return home. I do not remember the words, but I will never forget his gesture of love.

He follows not only his parents' footsteps, but also his senior sister's. Emily once offered an eloquent prayer in front of my home congregation when she traveled with her parents. It would not surprise me if she, at three years old in 2004, prayed traveling mercies for her mommy's first trip to the United States.

Connections

Now you are the body of Christ, and each one of you is a part of it.

1 Corinthians 12:27

October 2004

Dr. Mercy's dream to travel to the United States finally came true. On a connecting flight through Europe, Dr. Mercy drifted in and out of sleep. She woke to hear the flight attendant politely give instructions to fasten seatbelts and put seats and tray tables in their upright position. Bending down, Dr. Mercy took her itinerary out of her purse.

Let's see, Dr. Mercy thought, I need to check my connection. I cannot miss it.

Dr. Mercy needed to get to the hospital in Austin, Texas, as quickly as possible to help a girl prepare for heart surgery not available in Nigeria. After a scheduling mix-up kept Dr. Mercy from traveling with two-year-old Sewuese and Sewuese's mother, Dr. Mercy now followed them by a few days.

God, are you sure that I am supposed to go after that flight mix-up? Help me figure my way around the airport to make my connecting flight. Please grant me safety, and thank you for safely carrying the girl and her mother earlier.

As Dr. Mercy waited for the airplane to land, she thought about Cori Stern, the young American woman who visited Faith Alive and started The Cradle of Life Foundation. Thanks to Cori's coordinated efforts with the Texas hospital, the nonprofit HeartGift, and a few other foundations, Sewuese's broken heart had a chance to be healed.

Thank you, God, for the gift of my own children that I did not know if I could have. She thought of Emily and Prince, safe at home with their daddy and their live-in help. It was not easy to be so far from her family, but she trusted God and her husband to protect the children.

After successfully making her connecting flight, she finally arrived in Texas and joined Seweuse at the hospital. Both the girl and her mother were struggling with high fevers, aches, and dry coughs.

"They must have caught a flu on the airplane," one of the doctors told Dr. Mercy.

"Or maybe it is malaria," she said. "It is not uncommon for Nigerians to get it, and the stress of this travel may have made it worse. Let me give them some of the anti-malarial medicine that I brought."

Fortunately, the medicine worked quickly. Dr. Mercy stayed with them about two weeks, enough time to monitor Sewuese's health through a delayed but successful surgery.

While in Texas, Dr. Mercy connected with HeartGift Foundation's Executive Director, Teri O'Glee. They commiserated over the thousands of Nigerians who died each year because they lacked access to specialized treatments and surgeries. Dr. Mercy told Teri about the minor surgeries for appendicitis, hernias, and prostates that she regularly and voluntarily performed at Faith Alive in addition to her full-time surgical residency at JUTH. She sometimes performed surgeries with the aid of a headlamp if the generator stopped powering lights as well as with the aid of a finger pulse sensor and oximeter.

"So many Nigerians lose hope if they discover they or their children have cancer or heart diseases," Dr. Mercy told Teri. "Without adequate facilities or skills, it is as if doctors send people home to write their wills or buy their children's caskets. And AIDS. That is the same. At Faith Alive, we are waiting to receive some promised antiretroviral medications to bring people back to life."

"Who promised what, exactly?" Teri asked.

"There is a program that your government, the United States government, has started. It is called PEPFAR: President's Emergency Plan for AIDS Relief." Mercy continued, explaining that Faith Alive was the first faith-based nonprofit in Nigeria to be accepted. She said that PEPFAR committed to send Faith Alive enough antiretroviral medications (ARVs) to treat the first 2,000 patients there whose

HIV had worsened to full-blown AIDS. "But we have not received any ARVs yet. The longer we wait, more people will die."

"That's awful," Teri said. "I've heard of PEPFAR... yes, I have a friend, and I think he knows a top official in that department." A woman of action, Teri contacted her friend Tim, a retired attorney. The three of them sat down for lunch a few days later.

Not expecting anything from this lunch except good conversation and food, Dr. Mercy answered Tim's questions. PEPFAR was new at the time so they started talking about how the program would work.

Tim asked if Dr. Mercy, as an educated Nigerian practitioner, thought that PEPFAR was do-able and welcomed in Nigeria.

"Yes and yes!" she said.

Tim seemed encouraged. "If it'll be possible and I can arrange it, would you like to meet the PEPFAR director?"

With widening eyes, Mercy looked at Teri who nodded yes, this is true. "Of course, please," said Dr. Mercy. Little did she know where that meeting would occur.

The next day, Dr. Mercy answered her phone. "Hallo?"

"Dr. Mercy? This is Tim."

"Yes?"

"Do you have your passport with you?" he asked.

"You mean my passport photo? Do you need my photo?" Dr. Mercy asked, thinking that the PEPFAR director needed something official to screen credentials.

"No, your passport."

"Uh, yes…but why?"

"Because," Tim said, "you will need it to fly to the White House in Washington, D.C."

Dr. Mercy hesitated. She had never even visited Aso Rock, Nigeria's equivalent to the White House. "Have I done something wrong?"

"No." Tim laughed. "You are doing things right. My friend Joe O'Neill, a director there, wants to meet you. You are a critical connector to our end-users. Can you work a visit into your schedule?"

"Thank you," she said. "I would very much like to go. But I will need to make arrangements. May I call you back?"

"Of course," he said. "I look forward to it."

After they hung up, she had to sit down.

God, is this real? Someone at the American White House wants to talk with me? Who am I? But if you want me to go, please make a way.

Still unsure, she called her American friend Sally Barlow, U.S. Coordinator at the time for Faith Alive. Sally's partner Pam had met Dr. Chris in Albuquerque during his 1996 visit, and she and Sally got heavily involved with Drs. Chris and Mercy after visiting Faith Alive. Sally made a few calls to confirm the offer's validity. Believing that this rare opportunity for Dr. Mercy needed to occur, Sally and Pam paid Dr. Mercy's airfare and arranged for their friend Nanci Sebeniecher to host Dr. Mercy on the East Coast.

With this string of connections and blessing from her husband, Dr. Mercy flew to Washington, D.C.

She saw lines of tourists as she approached the White House. This is not like Aso Rock, she thought, where people dare not approach this casually.

Taking it all in, she prayed. *God, am I really seeing this? I, who was denied a visa in 1999 and thereafter even to visit America, am now a guest at the White House. Only you, God. Not me. Only by your design.*

After security scanned her body and purse, Dr. Mercy received a nametag to wear around her neck. With American escorts, she walked into Margaret Spellings's office where she met the secretary of domestic affairs and Dr. Joseph O'Neill, the medical director and deputy coordinator in the Office of the U.S. Global AIDS Coordinator.

Dr. Mercy marveled at the large, oval conference table, American flag, a picture of the president, and various global souvenirs. Similar to the movies, she thought, only more regal in person.

Secretary Spellings invited everyone to sit at the conference table for their meeting. Dr. Mercy gently pulled back a chair and sat down. She thought they would ask her a few questions, but they wanted to know everything. How did Faith Alive begin? What was its vision? How many patients there were HIV-positive? How many needed to be on ARVs right away? How many died from AIDS complications, and how many more did she anticipate?

After Dr. Mercy answered the questions as thoroughly and honestly as possible, they asked, "What is the biggest problem at Faith Alive?"

Dr. Mercy did not hesitate.

"When I go to bed at night," she said pensively, "I remember how the patients look at me." She paused. "They ask when the drugs are coming. I have no answer to give them. I just pray that these drugs get to them and their children."

Silence.

Visibly touched, the group assured her that they would personally make sure that the ARVs got to Faith Alive.

Thank you, God. May it be so.

After her time in Washington, D.C., Dr. Mercy continued her scheduled six-week tour of the United States to meet with people who had heard about Faith Alive via word of mouth or visited. She witnessed surgeries and talked with physicians at Johns Hopkins Hospital and University of New Mexico Hospital. Audiences from Boston University on the East Coast to Bayside Covenant Church in Granite Bay on the West Coast heard her speak about Faith Alive and medical conditions in Nigeria. Many of them, moved by her intelligence and honesty, donated money and medical supplies.

In early December, it came time for Dr. Mercy to return home. As she waited to board the airplane, she anticipated her connecting flights. The process reminded her of all the connections from God that had taken her across America and to the White House. Like ligaments and joints, each link worked together to complete a healthy body.

God, I do not believe in coincidences. You orchestrate and arrange things, working ahead of me to put into place the path I must take to do your will. Thank you for blessing me, and Faith Alive, with this expanding international family.

When she arrived home in Nigeria, she hugged her children and greeted her husband. She had so many stories to tell, so much good news to share. The upcoming holiday break would allow time to exchange information. She had Christmas gifts from America for her family, priceless memories to share, and a vision for Nigeria to advance its surgical capabilities.

But the best gifts that Christmas were Sewuese's repaired heart and the boxes that greeted Dr. Mercy at Faith Alive—ARVs for more than 2,000 patients.

● ● ●

By 2012, PEPFAR's support increased to cover nearly 4,000 HIV-positive patients. However, given the economic downturn and United States' budget cuts, continued support for Faith Alive is not guaranteed. I am concerned about what will happen to the patients if the United States reduces or withdraws its financial support.

Remembering God's faithfulness in the creation and rebuilding of Faith Alive, however, gives me hope for its future.

part
2

FAITH ALIVE
HOSPITAL

A successful founder makes God-sized goals, listens for God's voice, and trusts God when things get rough.

Dr. Chris standing amid burned Faith
Alive building, April, 2006

New Faith Alive Hospital, June, 2009

God-Sized Goals

Jesus looked at them and said, 'With man this is impossible, but with God all things are possible.'

Matthew 19:26

August 2011

Friday evening's darkness descended on the people of Jos. Night usually lured wayward youth to drinking establishments and promiscuity. But the bomb explosion at the United Nations' building in Nigeria's capital, Abuja, cast a somber mood over the upcoming weekend. Many people chose that August Friday in 2011 to stay close to their homes, considering the situation too dangerous to gather in crowded public places.

Six men and two women, disturbed but not deterred by the day's events, gathered for their weekly mentoring class at Faith Alive. They arrived over a ten-minute span that allowed enough time for the security guards to move metal detection wands over and inside each of their backpacks or purses. Dr. Chris came last, rushing from his wife's birthday dinner. Apologizing to his mentees, he led them up two levels of stairs to the meeting room, past the mural of a dark-skinned Jesus leaning down to help someone on bended knee.

They settled into padded, wooden chairs with attached writing surfaces. Wanting to release them at 8:30 p.m., just fifty minutes later, Dr. Chris wasted no time beginning his review of the material they had covered over the past weeks. Verbal repetition, he believed, was a great teaching method, especially in this largely oral culture.

"What three elements need to be part of your life mission statement?" he asked.

Knowing from experience that their teacher expected recall, a fashionable young woman in her twenties spoke first. "A target, strength, and…" she said, glancing at her notes, "a desired change."

"Excellent!" Dr. Chris said as if she had just answered the winning question on the internationally known *Who Wants to be a Millionaire*. He then said, "Think of John 3:16. Let us say it together."

"For God so loved the world that he gave his one and only Son," they recited, "that whosoever believes in him shall not perish but have eternal life."

"Good," he said. "Now, what is God's target?"

"The world," a young man wearing jeans and a T-shirt said.

"Correct. And what strength did he use?"

Nobody spoke, but Dr. Chris saw his youngest male student flip through a well-worn Bible. Not hearing an immediate answer, Dr. Chris said, "His Son. He gave His one and only Son. Now, what is God's desired change?"

Dr. Chris smiled widely and nodded when the young woman wearing stylish glasses said, "Eternal life."

"Yes, yes," he confirmed. "Our lives' missions, too, need to have a target, a strength, and a desired change. The ones you have written and turned in are good. Next, we need to have goals to accomplish our missions. Who remembers what G-O-A-L stands for?" He looked around the room and said, "Let us say it together."

The class, eager to please their mentor, recited aloud, "G:God-honoring, O:objective, A:ambitious, L:life-enhancing."

"Good. And why does it need to be ambitious?" he asked them.

"Sir," the middle-aged man sitting off to the side said, "so that only God gets the glory."

"You are correct!" Dr. Chris beamed. "So that no man can take the credit. If it is within our reach, then we can say that we did it. But if it is an unrealistic goal, something so big, then it can only be God who does it. And it requires that we have faith in God to provide."

Pointing to the papers on their desks, he said, "Look at your goal, the one that you brought tonight. Turn to the person sitting next to you and spend a few minutes telling each other how yours has all four parts of G-O-A-L."

His students, the ones he had carefully chosen based on their application essays, discussed in pairs. Over the murmur of their voices, Dr. Chris's mind drifted back to his own ambitious goal fifteen years earlier—to start Faith Alive.

He had rooted his goal in a deal he made with God when he was much younger, the last-born of his carpenter father and mother's ten children. They suffered to earn enough money for food and school. Dr. Chris told God that if God would take his family out of poverty, he would grow up to serve the poor. However, not until 1996 during his three-month medical fellowship in Albuquerque, New Mexico, did he begin envisioning Faith Alive.

It was the first time he had visited the United States, a place many Nigerians consider to be the land of milk and honey. While he enjoyed the smooth streets, clean air, and constant flow of water and electricity, he missed the community of his homeland. People in the United States did not mingle while fetching water, hanging laundry, or walking to the market. Americans only greeted each other on the street with a nod or to say "hi" while rushing to get somewhere.

Dr. Chris's loneliness began to lift when he met Dick Linderman. When their conversation turned to God, Dr. Chris shared his desire to worship with other Christians.

"Come to our church," Dick said. "There are only five of us who meet in someone's home as Emmanuel International Church pastored by Barbara Gould, but you are more than welcome."

Dr. Chris eagerly anticipated the next Sunday. When the Christian Sabbath finally came, he took his Bible and met the others. One woman, Christa Barnes, spoke passionately about loving God and hearing messages from him. When she prayed, her body responded with sudden shudders as if God's power infused her body. Dr. Chris, from a culture respectful of prophets, sensed her special connection to God.

When she prophesized that God wanted a young man in the room to do something great for God, he knew she spoke about him. The others confirmed it by anointing him with oil, praying, and collecting an offering. He humbly accepted their $30 and challenge to discern God's call for significance.

Wanting to meet more Christians and experience a larger American congregation, Dr. Chris asked Dick to recommend another church. So Dr. Chris went to Living Faith Church Alive—Albuquerque led by the Rev. Larry Poe. Compared to the home church with five people, Rev. Poe's church seemed large with fifty or sixty members. After meeting Dr. Chris at a worship service, many congregants showered him with love by visiting his apartment, giving him rides, and taking him meals. The comfort and fellowship tasted good.

One Sunday, a church leader asked the congregation to raise their hands if they wanted to do great things for God. With Christa's prophetic words embedded in his mind, Dr. Chris shot his hand straight up as if he might actually touch the hem of heaven.

Yes, Lord, I want to do great things for you! I commit myself to be available for you, whatever you want me to do.

He continued to seek God's guidance. As his study months ended, Larry approached Dr. Chris with a generous offer—a permanent and comfortable life in New Mexico. His immigration chances were good in 1996, and the temptation was great. But Dr. Chris felt no peace about living in the United States. Americans already had advanced health care. Nigerians desperately needed trained doctors to care for so many of their own people struggling in abject poverty.

Respecting and admiring Dr. Chris's decision, Rev. Poe and his church took a special offering for Dr. Chris. They gave him the entire sum—$303—and a promise of continued prayer support. Combined with the home church's offering, Dr. Chris left Albuquerque with $333, blessings, and an obedience to stay true to the deal he had made with God many years earlier.

As the airplane crossed the wide sea between continents, Dr. Chris prayed. *I am coming home. Now, what great thing do you want me to do?* The song, "I Call Him Faithful, I Call Him Savior," ran through his mind, the lyrics encouraging him.

Settling back into his full-time work at JUTH that April in 1996, Dr. Chris noticed a magazine article that he had saved years earlier. He looked with new interest at the title, "What can one Christian Doctor do for the Poor?" He wondered if the title provided a clue to his life mission. Below the headline, he read the prompt to imagine an ailing president of a country rushed to a hospital. A doctor there would leave everything to attend to the president, not asking first for proof of payment.

Dr. Chris continued reading the article. The author told him that we have the presence of our president, Jesus Christ, who comes to us in the form of the hungry and sick. He visits our hospitals daily. How then, the writer asked, will we respond?

The challenge pointed directly at Dr. Chris and transformed into a vision. A hospital. Treating everyone as if they were Jesus. A hospital not charging money for the poorest of the poor.

But how? God, I only have $333!

One voice in his head said, "Trust God and do it," while the other voice said, "It is not possible." Dr. Chris agonized over the contrast between realism and faith, wrestling anxiously for about a week.

He remembered Christa's prophecy and his raised hand to do something great for God. At the end of a week's time, he had a constant and strong sense of God saying, "I have given you all the resources you need." Dr. Chris surrendered.

It does not seem possible. But God, I make myself available. Please do whatever you want with me.

Whenever he envisioned the hospital, he knew that medical, social, and spiritual services were necessary for healing. Without a detailed, long-term strategic plan, Dr. Chris started by faith. He shared his vision with Dr. Bala Takaya, a supportive friend. He donated ten years' rent, at no cost to Dr. Chris, for an available four-room flat on the second level of 6C Tafawa Balewa Street in a busy section of Jos.

With accomodations provided, Dr. Chris spent his $333 on a table, chairs, and other items. When he shared his vision and good news with Larry in Albuquerque, Larry made a donation for other start-up costs. Dr. Chris soon had enough money to hang his shingle.

On June 23, 1996, two months after leaving the United States where he had said "yes" to God, Dr. Chris posted a sign to the building's rusted railing. He wanted to use part of the name of Larry's church, but Jos already had a church named Living Faith. So Dr. Chris modified the title. Afraid of proclaiming that this was, or would become, a full-fledged hospital, the sign simply said, "Faith Alive Counseling Center."

He waited.

Not wanting to be idle, Dr. Chris spent the first few evenings at the center preparing for clients after his JUTH job. Early the third evening, an inquisitive young woman's eye spotted the sign. Naomi had lived a few blocks away for many years and had never before seen that sign. With a strange pull toward the stairs, she did not know where else to turn for help about her serious personal problems. So she took a first step. Then a second.

Nearing the top step, Naomi spotted a man bent over a short broom sweeping the floor. He looked up and smiled, saying excitedly, "You are welcome." He put the broom down and motioned for her, saying, "Come. Come in and sit."

Skeptical, she sat down and listened as this man introduced himself as Dr. Chris. Sensing despair in her voice and heart, he read Psalm 13, a prayer for help, and Isaiah 41:18 & 19, God's promise to turn the dry land into flowing springs. But Naomi needed more visits before she could trust Dr. Chris, trust the Christian books and magazines he lent her, and trust that he cared and could help.

Still not convinced of his sincerity, she stopped coming. Dr. Chris worried about her, so he went looking for her. Only after that did she believe his integrity.

Dr. Chris offered Naomi housing and financial assistance to graduate and eventually pursue university studies. Her life began to improve, and soon she volunteered for Faith Alive. She did not take a salary for the next ten years from the person and the place that gave her hope for a better future.

Not long after she first ventured up the counseling center's steps in 1996, others started to trickle in. Dr. Chris listened to their cries about depression, finances, and marital problems. An increasing number of them shared a compounding health problem. Many of their troubles—families abandoning them, spouses dying, fathers fired from their jobs or too sick to work, children left orphaned—stemmed from HIV/AIDS. At that time, the necessary drugs were much too expensive, so Dr. Chris offered what he could—vitamins, Bible verses, and prayer.

Wishing that he could offer more advanced medical services, Dr. Chris prayed. *Lord, what will we do for our people?*

Fifteen years later, during the evening of this mentoring class, Dr. Chris silently reflected on God's answer. God had been faithful amid setbacks, trials, and even a fire that threatened to destroy Dr. Chris's optimism and continued growth—both his and Faith Alive's.

But he chose hope. And with God, he shared that hope with thousands of people, including those infected or affected by the HIV virus, in the form of holistic care. After all, this day in 2011 he stood on the third floor of this modern, three-story building, state-of-the-art by Nigerian standards. His one-man show had grown into a staff of 150—from medical doctors to maintenance to volunteers. Thanks to funding over the years from partnerships with individuals, churches, and agencies around the world, as well as their biggest contributor, the U.S. government's PEPFAR program, Faith Alive has served more than 10,000 patients free of charge. More than 4,000 of those with HIV/AIDS received lifesaving medications.

Faith Alive's services included doctors' visits, surgeries, counseling, prayer, discipleship lessons, HIV-positive support group and awareness education, transitional housing, emergency food and clothing, micro lending, children's school scholarships, Kiddies' Club, school, satellite clinics, and skills-training like sewing, knitting, using a computer, and driving.

Soon he would tell his mentoring class the truth. That he had not originally intended to specialize in HIV/AIDS. That he was ashamed that he started a small counseling center when God wanted a full-scale hospital.

"Wa-oh," he will say. "Before my very eyes, I see this great God proving me a liar and himself true and faithful. Every word our great God said has come to pass."

His life mission, he will share, has two intended targets: the less privileged and medical students in Nigeria. "I want to equip people to make a difference in others' lives rather than being enticed by the material gains of the medical profession," he will say, realizing that many Nigerian doctors and nurses prefer to spend their earnings on fancy cars and homes or practice their skills abroad. He will add that he wants to use his medical skills and deep faith for a desired change— to give people the opportunity to make a decision for Jesus Christ.

Next, he will tell his students about his even bigger goal, one based on his training at the Mayo Clinic in Rochester, Minnesota, in 1999. "My desire," he will say to his class as he has said to many people, "is to make Faith Alive a 'Mayo' in Africa for Christian doctors, nurses, and health care personnel. It will be a Christian medical school that will make disciples of medical and paramedical people to reach more for God." And then, as if this is not enough, he will add to his God-honoring, objective, ambitious, and life-enhancing goal. "And duplication of this ministry all over Africa and indeed his entire territory: the world—both physically and in the hearts of all men and women."

But he does not have to tell his mentees about all of this tonight. He will teach them during other evening sessions to pray specifically, consistently, intelligently, and regularly—with expectancy—for their ambitious goals. Maybe he will even use the fire as an example. But for tonight, they will learn how to listen to God's voice and start bold projects with a faith in God's provision. All they have to do is follow the same God who will lead them, and Nigeria, to a brighter future.

●　　●　　●

One other person sat in Dr. Chris's mentoring class that evening: me. I went to observe but instead benefitted as much as his other mentees. He asked them to get into groups of three people—one to tell his or her goal, one to play the role of an encouraging angel, and one to pretend to be the devil.

I listened as a man shared his goal of writing and publishing a Christian book. The angel told him how much God loved him, how all things with God are possible, and how God will direct and guide his path. The devil interspersed hissing words that the mentee was not good enough, he would be wasting his time, and that his book would not make a difference in anyone's life.

Unknown to that mentee, I had already written a rough draft of this book. I had heard and answered God's call to write but also struggled with a lack of confidence that anyone would buy or read my words. Granted, I majored in English literature and minored in journalism and sociology many years ago in college, but spending three years to write and publish a top-quality book that honored God seemed far beyond my ability. Only God's strength would get me through. Thanks to the exercise in Dr. Chris's class, I prepared for obstacles, both internal and external, by listening to the angel.

I will continue to keep my eyes on Jesus, just as Dr. Chris did when he experienced a striking setback in 2006.

Out of the Ashes

*The God of heaven will give us success; therefore
we his servants will arise and build...the strength
of the laborers is giving out...we cannot rebuild
the wall...there is so much rubble...we continued
to work...the wall was completed...with the help
of our God.*

Nehemiah 2-6 excerpts

April 13, 2006

Dr. Chris and his children enjoyed a few days in Abuja,
hours away from Faith Alive in Jos, waiting to pick up
international visitors Ryan Day and his wife Hillary
Lum. Deep in sleep early one morning, the guesthouse's
ringing telephone woke him.

"My dear," he heard his wife say with a defeated
tone. She paused before recounting the situation at
Faith Alive.

He heard her descriptions but focused on the main points. The call around midnight. Speeding to the hospital. Joining neighbors as they rushed to fetch water from nearby wells, throwing bucketfuls through the thick smoke into the raging inferno. The smell of burning and fear. Rumors of a power surge in the lab, a rat's nest of wires, sparking the blaze. Hearing debris crackling. Firefighters hosing the perimeter, defending the surrounding buildings from jumping flames. Neighbors rallying in defense of Faith Alive and their properties to create their own bucket brigade with the firefighters.

Hearing of the fire's severity, Dr. Chris wanted to return to Jos immediately. Yet he knew that hazardous road conditions and threats of armed robbers rendered it dangerous for travel before the sun rose. Even if he risked the journey, the fire's embers would be cold before he returned.

"God will help us through this, somehow." Dr. Chris comforted his wife, Dr. Mercy. "The children and I will return right away."

"There is no need, really," she said. "I can manage here. The children enjoy Abuja, and we will be together this Sunday for Easter."

Yes, Easter, Dr. Chris thought. And today was Maundy Thursday. How fitting. With time to reflect from a distance, Dr. Chris drew parallels between the darkness of both Jesus' crucifixion and the fire. Both gave him reasons to grieve about this life on Earth, to slip into doubting God's faithfulness.

Three days later, Dr. Chris stood in the ashy
rubble where his lab at Faith Alive had been four
days earlier. His wife was right when she said that the
fire had destroyed nearly everything in one of the old
buildings, just a few steps away from the new building's
construction. This old building, now without a roof,
exposed its rooms like a maze. It was carpeted with
blackened medical files and papers, twisted corrugated
metal, and melted equipment. Tangled wires draped
loosely around beams and hung from walls, exposed
during one of the hottest months in Jos. What the fire
had not destroyed, buckets of water had.

Being here this day—smelling the dank ashes,
touching the charcoaled walls, seeing the destruction—
made it real. They had lost so much. In addition to the
overcrowded physical space for seeing patients, all of
the important lab equipment burned. Thousands of
patients' medical histories had gone up with the smoke,
fueled by the wooden tables with etchings inadvertently
marked beneath written prescriptions.

Shuffling through the mess, Dr. Chris tilted back
his head. Squinting through the sun beaming through
the open ceiling, he gazed up at the new Faith Alive
building under construction a few yards away. Only a
walkway not big enough for a small car separated the
charred, one-story building from the emerging, three-
story one.

Continuing the parallels he saw on Maundy
Thursday, Dr. Chris marveled at the Easter
resurrection—both for the Lord and Faith Alive. He
recalled that after Jesus' resurrection, the angel at the

tomb asked the women why they looked among the dead for the one alive.

Oh, God, you are faithful. Amid the destruction, you are already creating new life, something much bigger and better than we can imagine. Shall we receive the good at your hand and not receive the bad also? I do not know why this has happened. But I know that you are a great and faithful God. With you, after death there is resurrection.

Looking down again at the mess, he started to tally what remained. Most important: human lives. No patients or staff died during the fire. Medications, especially the expensive ones that HIV-positive patients needed to take daily or risk developing a deadly resistance, were safe in the adjoining pharmacy. Only a few of the patients' paper medical files could be recovered, but other data stored on a computer in the remaining one-story building survived. The fire had not reached the main generator, along with stored propane and diesel, which could have exploded into the new building.

Dr. Chris thanked God for members of Bayside Covenant Church in California who visited Faith Alive during the last few years and decided to do something about the overcrowded conditions. They had returned to their church and held a successful fundraising campaign for Faith Alive's new building. With the help of Dr. Chris's longtime friend, Amos the architect, they broke ground in late 2005 directly next to the old buildings. Now the new one would need to be finished as soon as possible.

Dr. Chris and Amos figured out a plan. Instead of working regular hours, they needed to labor around the clock. Soon, a line of men, women, and older youth waited at a table by the street each morning to be hired alongside Faith Alive staff. The generator roared through the days and nights as a string of workers formed a human chain to transport supplies from the street to the third floor. Women in long skirts, flip flops, and scarves tied around their heads to protect their hair steadied large, metal bowls of wet concrete as they walked up two flights of stairs.

Inspired by the biblical Nehemiah, whose compassion for his hurting people compelled him to rebuild the temple, Dr. Chris encouraged the workers.

"Rely on God," Dr. Chris told the workers when they did not see all the supplies that they needed. "God will provide."

"Refuse to give up," he said when he heard rumblings of frustration or fatigue. "Go home and rest, but we need you tomorrow."

"Remember what is important," he reminded himself when fears or thoughts of failure crept into his mind. He kept his Bible close, frequently rereading Nehemiah to sustain his spirit. If Nehemiah and his crew could overcome doubts and adversity to complete the wall in just fifty-two days with God's help, surely the new Faith Alive building would be ready soon.

When the roof covered the third floor two months later, Dr. Chris stood there and looked out of the blue-tinted windows. With a bird's eye view, he saw an outline of the charred building below. Later, he thought, we will raze that building for a courtyard and two-story building. Looking to the horizon, he saw the flat a few blocks away where he had originally hung the "Faith Alive Counseling Center" sign. He turned his head to the right a bit and saw their transitional housing down the street.

Wow, God. You are faithful. I think we are ready to dedicate this new building to you and move in.

On June 25, 2006, ten years to the day after his first client had walked into the Faith Alive Counseling Center, Dr. Chris opened the new hospital building's doors. Hundreds of people filled the Faith Alive Hospital with robust praise songs and prayers of thanksgiving. As he stood on the clean concrete floor, he raised his hands and looked toward heaven. Then he spoke into the microphone.

"Hear now our Dedication Declaration," he said. "We have gathered to declare that we will refuse to settle for less than God's best. Therefore, we make the following affirmations." Pointing to their programs, he indicated for them to join him. He led them in unison, "I am confident in God's promises, I am committed to God's purposes, and I am committed to God's people."

●   ●   ●

Since that Easter, Dr. Chris vividly remembers standing among the ashes in 2006. Even though so much of their past work had been destroyed, he understands why the new building's construction had been in process before the fire. Dr. Chris knows firsthand that God's power is at work to give us resurrection hope when we stand among death and destruction.

Let me introduce you to some of the people at Faith Alive who share his living faith.

part
3

FAITH ALIVE STAFF

Tell me someone is a Christian, and I will believe it by seeing the lives he has touched.

Dr. Chris with Faith Alive staff and volunteers, 2006

Architect for God

But thanks be to God! He gives us the victory
through our LORD *Jesus Christ. Therefore, my*
dear brothers, stand firm. Let nothing move you.
Always give yourselves fully to the work of the
LORD, *because you know that your labor in the*
LORD *is not in vain."*

1 Corinthians 15:57 & 58

1992

Thirty-nine-year-old Amos Toye closed his eyes but
sleep eluded him. If only he could drift away on this
long commute and wake up in Bauchi State. He shifted
his legs to get comfortable in the taxi's front seat. He
sat under the rearview mirror, crammed between the
driver and another passenger. At least he was not one
of the four people in the middle seat or the three others
in the back of the small, green station wagon.

Instead of squeezing in a few more passengers to
face backward, sideways, up or down, the driver saved

space for containers of fuel. The Nigerian gas shortage rendered it nearly impossible to fill up on the trip between Plateau State and Bauchi State. Amos was used to smelling other people's body odor on this hot day, but constricted his nostrils to block out the fuel's strong smell.

He tried to focus his thoughts on his wife and two young children. He remembered that providing for them was the reason he sometimes commuted for hours to work as an architect. Someday he would find a job closer to his home in Jos, own a vehicle to drive his family to and from church, and make a way for his children to attend university.

Amos looked out the taxi's front window until the landscape changed from homes and businesses to acres upon acres of fertile green fields at the foot of steep hills. The driver sped faster now as the sun faded, impatiently passing slower-moving cars and trucks overflowing with cattle. Amos felt dizzy each time the driver swerved back into the right lane after narrowly escaping contact with oncoming traffic. They passed a stranded, mangled vehicle on the side of the road that had not been so lucky.

Normally the taxi's constant "beep, beep, beep" provided an almost musical backdrop to this lengthy ride. But today it combined with the smell of fuel to give Amos a headache. He asked the passenger on his right to roll the window down a little before Amos closed his eyes and felt some relief. Maybe now, like the receding sun, he would be able to put the day to rest. He closed his eyes and drifted to sleep.

Amos jolted awake when he heard the driver shout. He saw a pair of headlights headed straight for them. The taxi driver tried to swerve, but there was not enough time. A head-on crash launched them into the bush and exploded the fuel into a raging inferno.

Gasping for breath, Amos felt the heat and flames rising from the car floor. They pierced his legs, his hands, his soul. His primal instinct kicked in.

Survive. Get out of the taxi. Or am I already outside?

He began desperately fighting the consuming fire with his jacket, swatting at the flames.

Are the other people screaming, or is this shrieking sound coming from my own mouth?

In the madness of the moment, he did not know if he was already dead or still alive. Thinking this to be his last prayer, he prayed.

Lord, I commit my life unto your hands.

Then he realized that he was outside of the car, free from the violent orange fire now lighting the black of night. Amos looked down and glimpsed his raw, seared skin falling away like peeling paint. Fortunately, the shock protected his nerves from realizing the pain's full impact. At least for now.

Help me, God! I do not want to die. My wife, my children. They need me. Please, please, please.

With every ounce of strength he could muster, Amos trudged toward the road. But no headlights approached.

Just stillness.

Resigned, he had only enough energy left to sit down on the road, raise his hands to heaven, and wait.

Before long, a convoy of military vehicles from Bauchi approached and stopped. The governor, on his way out of Jos, asked one of his men to take Amos back to Jos to JUTH. A few of his men carefully helped Amos into the back of one of their vehicles and laid him down.

On the way to the hospital, Amos remained conscious enough to give the driver his contact information.

"I shall not die, I shall live," he gasped. "God took me out of the fire and brought you to save me."

He closed his eyes and drifted in and out of consciousness.

At the hospital, doctors and nurses rushed Amos to surgery. They carefully removed his burnt skin and synthetic trousers that had melted onto his legs. His torso, feet, and chin were his only body parts not burned.

Coming out of anesthesia, Amos opened his eyes in time to see his wife, Asabe, before she collapsed on the cement floor. She had come to his side as soon as she heard the news but was not prepared for what awaited her. This charred, shriveled, bandaged man with third degree burns on 55 percent of his body did not resemble her tall, handsome husband of six years. Both of them needed time to accept this new reality.

Over the next few weeks, many of his friends visited to encourage and pray with Amos and Asabe. The man who had driven Amos to the hospital that fateful night also visited. When Amos realized who stood near his bed, he said, "Thank you, thank you, thank you. God sent you to save me." Then Amos paused, already sensing in his heart the next answer. "Did any other people survive the accident?"

"Oh, sir, I am so glad that you survived," he said. Then he looked down and added, "Unfortunately…the others did not. Only you lived through the fire."

Unable to turn his face away from the man because of neck burns, Amos closed his eyes and grimaced. He took a minute to gather his strength.

Oh, God in heaven, comfort their families. It is truly a miracle that I am alive. You must have something more for me to do here in this life.

Another day, Dr. Chris visited Amos at the hospital, the first of many times during Amos' recovery.

"My dear brother in Christ," Dr. Chris said to his close friend since university. "God will surely bring you through this. It is good that you are named Toye, 'something that survives, something that overcomes suffering.' You were right to shorten your name from Oguntoye, to remove the Ogun that does not glorify God. You will live, my friend. You will live."

During the next four months, Asabe relied on God's strength to help nurse Amos' infections, dressings, and bed sores. She encouraged him through his agonizing pain and sobs to relearn how to sit, stand, and eventually walk on his own two scarred legs after months of lying on his back. The first time he sat upright again, he thought the drab room had been turned upside down. In reality, the accident had rearranged more than his visual perspective.

Amos endured four months of extreme highs and lows, both physical and spiritual, before being released from the hospital to recover at home. With confidence that God would give him strength to heal, Amos faithfully followed all of the doctor's instructions. He soaked his body for an hour each day in warm salt water.

During those twelve months of recovery in the hospital and at home, Amos spent many hours reflecting.

"If God wanted me to die," Amos told Dr. Chris during another visit, "I would have died in that accident. God was helping me."

"Yes," Dr. Chris agreed. "God is as faithful to you now as he has been throughout your life. Remember university."

Amos did. His father had not had enough money to send Amos to the university, so Amos spent two years as an evangelist with Calvary Ministry. His heart ached for Hausa-speaking Muslims to know Jesus Christ. The evangelists traveled to various places in Nigeria to eat, sleep, and have open-air crusades.

After Calvary, Amos' spiritual mentor had just enough money for Amos to register for classes at the University of Jos. While he did not know how he could possibly afford ongoing costs, he felt honored to begin with a federal merit award scholarship; he would trust God to provide.

Waiting in the university's registration line, he struck up a conversation with a new medical student, Christian Isichei. Chris instantly treated Amos like a brother by inviting him for meals and going together to a Christian student fellowship and the nearby mountains to pray.

The school year progressed, but Amos' mathematics scores did not. He felt so discouraged that on the last day of the semester, he walked toward the university exit for what he thought was the last time. He saw Chris at the gate of the university.

"My brother, where are you going?" Chris asked.

"I am leaving the university."

"But you must not do that," Chris said. "God wants to do something great through you."

Amos' reflections that summer on Chris's words brought much encouragement. Wow, he thought, I have a friend at the university who still wants to see me there.

That fall, he packed his things and returned to the university.

Amos did not have much money, and Chris knew it. Once in a while, Chris gave Amos things like meal tickets. Not yet married and with his own eager means, Chris shared his apartment with Amos and other students who could not afford rent.

The two friends decided to run for offices of their residence hall, Amos as treasurer and Chris as chairman. Like the biblical David competing against the giant Goliath, others mocked Chris for undertaking a seemingly impossible task. The other candidates were older, more experienced, and confident. However, each one became disqualified after being caught giving and taking illegal campaign tokens or bribes. Chris won, unopposed, as chairman of Bauchi Hall. He joined Amos who was the newly elected treasurer.

With another friend, Amos and Chris started a magazine called "The Reminder." It encouraged Christian students to stay strong in their faith amid the typical campus atmosphere and not have their faith choked to death like seeds sown among thorns. The magazine reminded students of God's faithfulness in the Bible and in their own families. Amos and Chris scraped together enough funds to finance and distribute the magazine for free, taking occasional donations from students who had a little extra to share.

Most students were drawn to Amos' cheerful, outgoing personality and admired his intelligence. But one student became fiercely jealous and resented Amos for raising the academic standard for scholarships. The evening before Amos' scholastic defense, the student stole Amos' final project. The staff knew and liked Amos, so they gave him another opportunity to present his defense. While he was allowed to complete his architecture degree, he was no longer eligible to graduate in his class's top tier of students.

Dr. Chris cheered as Amos went on to earn a master's degree and work in construction. The university eventually hired Amos as a teacher and provided housing for him, his wife, and their four children. They lived in the same university housing as Dr. Chris's family.

Amos had only been teaching at the university for a few years before the fiery car accident. Not long after recovering from the burns, he told Dr. Chris about a new covenant he had made with God.

"There was once a man," Amos told Dr. Chris, "a man who was baptized with his wallet still in his pocket. Before being dunked in the river, the pastor noticed the man's pocket still held the man's wallet. The pastor suggested that he remove the wallet so that it did not get wet. No, the man said that he and his money would be baptized together, that God wanted all of him."

"Amen," Dr. Chris said.

"God gave me the gifts to become an architect," Amos said. "So I made a covenant with God to volunteer my time and talent to build churches."

"Oh, that is good," Dr. Chris said. "Very good."

"And the churches will be top quality. God deserves a quality house."

Since that covenant, Amos designed eight large churches in Nigeria, one of which is Dr. Chris's United Baptist Church about a block away from Faith Alive.

Given Amos' love for Jesus, his architectural skills, and selfless service, it is no surprise that Dr. Chris turned to Amos when Faith Alive needed to expand in 2005. The hospital was not a church per se, but another type of house for God. The ministers were the doctors, and the parishioners were the patients.

"Some people," Dr. Chris told Amos, "may never set foot in a church. But everyone knows that they need a hospital and will go there at least once in their lives. Faith Alive can reach many people for Jesus Christ."

With that encouragement, Amos fervently designed a sturdy three-story hospital right next to the existing cluster of one-story buildings that burst at its seams with patients. With financing from Bayside Covenant

Church in Granite Bay, California, Amos managed the construction.

By early 2006, Faith Alive staff and patients watched Amos' team pour concrete and erect the new building's framework. Construction continued on schedule until April 13 when a power surge from the electric company led to a massive fire in the existing building.

Standing among the ashes and rubble, Amos and Dr. Chris turned their faces toward heaven. They remembered God's redemption in the midst of that car fire years earlier.

●　　●　　●

After Amos reviewed this chapter for accuracy about his life, he was silent. I thought that I had gotten something wrong or that he might be upset to remember his sufferings.

"Amos," I said tentatively. "Are you okay?"

He looked at me through misty eyes and said, "I have never seen my life in this way."

I waited, ready to apologize if I had re-traumatized him.

"God is so faithful," he said. "This makes me want to do even more for God."

Amos reminds me of other Faith Alive staff who have overcome horrific adversity and dedicated their lives to Jesus.

Positive Pastor

For we do not have a high priest who is unable to sympathize with our weaknesses...

Hebrews 4:15

2008

Pastor Esther looked directly at the fifty or so mostly male Nigerian pastors and their wives. She had heard enough facts during this five-day "HIV and the Church" training—it was time to get personal. In her commanding yet friendly voice she challenged her fellow pastors, "Will you marry a couple if you know that one or both of them are HIV-positive?"

Many of these religious leaders at the heart of African life squirmed in their white plastic chairs. The afternoon heat, fused with the question, caused some to sweat profusely. Anticipating their reluctance to answer honestly in the large group, Pastor Esther asked them to divide into smaller discussion groups. Ten as-yet-unidentified members of Faith Alive's

HIV-positive support group strategically blended into different groups.

Pastor Esther walked among the circles and heard many of the pastors and their wives say, "People with HIV are just going to die anyway. What is the use of getting married?" Others said, "It is their own fault that they are HIV-positive. They need to pay for their sins. We do not want those people in our churches infecting us."

Though expected, their judgment stung. Pastor Esther steeled herself and glanced at a few of Faith Alive's support group members. Their brave silence strengthened her resolve to remain patient.

After allowing ample time for discussion, Pastor Esther gathered everyone in one group again. It was time for her to reveal the challenging truth.

"Please, allow me to introduce a few of my friends," she said. "They are members of Faith Alive's weekly support group that I work with closely." She paused to intensify the moment. "All of them are HIV-positive. They are planning to marry or are newly married."

One by one, the same people who had only moments before sat next to and felt the unsympathetic hearts of many of the pastors and their wives came forward. Each support group member, nicely dressed and looking healthy, stood up and recounted painful stories of stigmatization and rejection by their Christian friends, families, pastors, and churches. Some had been thrown out of their homes. Others feared losing their jobs if employers discovered their status.

Yet each person talked about their future. Some talked about continuing their educations at universities or through the Faith Alive computer, sewing, and knitting classes. Others worked in hospitals and schools. They hoped to start families and raise healthy children, now possible with medications that could stop the virus from infecting their babies during pregnancy and while breastfeeding.

"My first family is Faith Alive," one young woman said. "I am accepted there. Even on the days when my body feels sick, my spirit is strong. They have done for me what my own church has not."

As the support group members spoke, Pastor Esther watched the pastors and their wives' eyes widen. Some dropped their jaws. Others looked down, too ashamed of the insensitive comments they had made just a few minutes earlier. Still others touched their own cheeks, wiping fallen tears of shame and embarrassment.

Pastor Esther's patience was rewarded. No lecture could match the intensity of this lesson. Yet she was not ready to reveal the whole truth—that she, a fellow pastor, also lived with HIV. Her story stayed locked in her memory for now.

Eleven years earlier, in 1997, Esther had extended her left hand toward the lab technician at JUTH during her prenatal visit. Her twenty-six-year-old body had experienced the same tenderness and swelling as her first two pregnancies. What differed was her tiredness from chasing around her boys, Love and Shegun. She winced when the technician's needle pricked her middle finger; Esther's blood flowed into a vial.

"You can go now," the technician said. Unknown to Esther, the routine prenatal western-blot blood test, which at that time took days to show results, included a check for HIV. Not for her benefit, but so that the medical staff would know to protect themselves with extra precautions during the delivery.

Esther gathered her boys and left the hospital. They returned a few days later to collect the results. The doctor told her that everything was fine. Perhaps he did not tell his patients about their HIV-positive status because no treatment was available; HIV at that time was a certain death sentence. Lifesaving antiretroviral medications were too costly for even the wealthiest people then, let alone the wife of a construction worker whose out-of-town jobs only allowed him to sleep at home one or two nights a month.

Esther sensed something in her doctor's voice that was not honest. Later, one of her friends who worked at that hospital visited Esther. The friend asked her if she wanted to know her blood test results. Yes! In her living room, with no counseling or advice about how to protect her baby, she learned the truth. HIV was mounting an assault on her family.

Paralyzed by this new reality, Esther did not hear the rain begin to fall outside, first like a friend knocking at the door but soon revealing its true identity—an unremorseful intruder, like HIV, indiscriminatingly saturating everything in its path.

When her husband, Ajibola, came home a few days later, she stopped weeping long enough to break the news.

"It cannot be," he said. "There is no such thing as HIV." Unlike Esther who did not doubt the virus, he believed that this so-called disease was a curse from witch doctors rather than a consequence of his behavior.

"You cannot be serious," she said. The temporary comfort of denial tempted her, but the reality expanded like her body's pregnancy. "Well," she said, "we will see."

Neither the news of her status nor her pregnancy deterred Ajibola's desire for his wife, who still looked healthy. When he lay on top of her in their bedroom at night, she prayed silently.

God, take away my anger and keep him away from other women. The children and I will need him now more than ever. You must be the one to work in his heart.

A few months later, they welcomed their new baby boy. They named him Testimony because Esther knew that this boy would be proof of something. Exactly what, she was unsure. He seemed like a typical baby until about six or seven months later when he started falling sick. People started to count his visibly protruding ribs.

"Madam," people would shout at Esther, "what happened to this your big baby? You cannot carry this thing anymore. This is no longer a human being."

Even Ajibola's extended family tried to convince him to give them the baby so that they could take him to the witch doctors. But Esther refused their offer to take the baby away to die at their merciless hands.

Dejected but resolute, Esther told her husband, "You are not going anywhere with this baby. This is my child, and I cannot throw him away. He is still breathing."

The next morning, when Love and Shegun were still asleep, she placed Testimony on the bed. Sobbing from angry desperation, she prayed.

God, I did not ask you for another child. You gave him to me. Why should I suffer for this child?

Gaining strength, she cried out. *God, either you do something about this boy's case or you take his life. Because from today henceforth I will not move an inch, and I am not giving him any medicine from the witch doctor. So, God, if he dies, I say it is you that the shame will go back to.*

Falling to her knees, she continued. *This embarrassment is too much for me to bear. God, you just do anything you want with him. But if you do not take his life now, then you must change his situation.*

Within a week or so, Testimony started to regain his appetite and then his energy. His cries got louder and his body bigger.

"Wow," people said, "this boy will survive it."

"Yes, he will," she said. Everyone but Esther looked dumbfounded. She knew that God had answered her prayers. At twenty months old, Testimony started to walk. Soon he ran behind his brothers.

He continued to grow, but Esther's husband started to fall ill on and off in 2001. The doctors tested him for various illnesses. When Esther asked him about his HIV test result, he did not tell her.

"It is positive, huh?" she asked. "Just tell me. I have already cried and cried for HIV, and I will not cry again."

"Yes," he said, confirming her suspicions.

With words powerful enough to be spoken quietly, she said, "You see where the lifestyle you have been living has landed you."

Silence.

Finally, he said, "But a man's body is not wood; a man cannot stay without a woman for long. It is hard to travel so much and be away from you."

When Esther did not validate her husband's defense, he said, "I am sorry. I am so sorry."

"The deed has been done already," she told him in a soft voice. "Just forget it. All you need to do is give your life to Christ and just make your ways right with him. I for one have forgiven you. It is for you to forgive yourself now and ask the Lord also to forgive you."

Ajibola hung his head as if he knew that his wife's grace and mercy were unmerited.

She continued, "I do not want to worry. Because if I keep that in my mind, I will keep worrying, and I will not be able to help you. You are sick now, and I would not be able to care for you. I would not be able to give you water to drink. It takes forgiveness for me to be able to take care of you the way I am supposed to, sitting close to you on your sickbed, and doing all the things I need to do."

From that day on, the two were inseparable.

Two or three days before he died, he told Esther, "This room is too bright."

She said, "Okay, should I drop the curtains?" She closed them.

"No," he said, "it is too bright." Esther put out the light.

Ajibola looked at her and smiled. He said, "You have eyes, but you cannot see. There is a glory in this room. There is a light that you cannot put off. It is shining. Kai, I am sorry for you, because you cannot see anything. Your eyes are just there. You cannot see."

Before he died by her side in November 2001, she told him, "I love you, but God loves you more. Go now."

Esther's earlier words were wrong about not having more tears for the tragedies that accompany HIV. She wept over her husband's death, a precursor to the coming tsunami of grief.

While their oldest son, Love, remained healthy and their youngest, Testimony, was growing strong, their middle son, Shegun, began to fall sick. He had been born prematurely and had been ill with tuberculosis and pneumonia as a toddler. Since then, however, he had grown normally.

"He is grieving the loss of his daddy," people said.

But Shegun's health rapidly declined. By August 2002, Ester admitted him to a hospital. A blood test revealed the all-too-familiar three letters: HIV. She was stunned.

His body continued to weaken. Try as he might, he could not fight the virus. Before long, he joined his daddy in heaven.

Esther's wails spoke volumes. In her heart, she wrestled with God.

Why would you allow something to happen to him? If I had known sooner that it was HIV, that boy would not have died. I could have done something. I never knew it was HIV. I did not know. It was too late. Oh, God, ohhhhhhhhhhh.

With a protective anger, Esther eventually collected herself enough to do what was necessary to nurture her other two sons.

A few months after Shegun's death, Esther needed to travel for church business. Her boys stayed with Esther's sister who noticed a rash on Testimony's body. She had heard of the Faith Alive Hospital and took him there. Dr. Chris examined Testimony and suspected the diagnosis; he counseled the aunt, believing her to be the child's mother.

Because test results at that time took a few days, Dr. Chris spoke with Esther's sister later that week. He said gently. "We did the test for your child as discussed, and he is positive for HIV. We would like for you to also be tested."

"Now hold on," Esther's sister said, "I am not the mother. The mother is my junior sister. When she comes back, I will ask her to see you."

When Esther returned to Jos, she did not want to go to Faith Alive. But Dr. Chris refused to treat Testimony without also treating his mother. So Esther went reluctantly. Dr. Chris counseled her about HIV and asked to test her for the virus.

"I already know," she told him.

Dr. Chris looked at her. "What do you know?"

"I know that I have HIV. I have taken the test before."

"Let us still do it again," he said, wanting to confirm the diagnosis before starting mother and child on some type of treatment. Faith Alive did not yet have easy access to lifesaving antiretroviral medications but did have antibiotics that helped ward off opportunistic infections like pneumonia and tuberculosis that preyed on weakened immune systems.

"With all pleasure," Esther said before taking the test, unconvinced that this doctor had anything to offer.

Dr. Chris sent her to the lab for testing, gave her Testimony's antibiotic medicine, and asked her to come back the next week. She did not.

God, I do not feel like going back. If HIV is going to kill me, let me die. I do not want to go to Faith Alive and have everyone looking at me like I am HIV-positive. I do not need anybody else's help. But…my son does.

She steeled her spirit and continued to wrestle with God during the next few months.

If you want me to be a pastor, why did you put HIV in my body? How can I be HIV-positive and still be talking to people about your word?

Finally, a thought came to her. *Jesus Christ had to come in the form of human beings. We do not have a high priest that does not feel what we feel. So, God, what is the meaning of that? I am not Jesus Christ. I am Esther!*

She sensed that God wanted her to know that she needed to go through what she was going through for her to be able to reach out to others. But, like the biblical Job, she tried to reason with God.

Ah, God, HIV is not enough? My husband, you took him. My son, you took him. All those things are not enough? Please, I have had enough.

"Yes," she heard a voice in her head say, "it is now time for you to move."

To where, now?

"Go to Faith Alive," the voice said. "I want you to strengthen those who are going through what you are going through." Then she remembered the man in John 9 who asked Jesus about a blind man. The man asked, "Who sinned, this man or his parents, that he was born blind?"

"Neither this man nor his parents sinned," said Jesus, "but this happened so that the work of God might be displayed in his life."

Finally trusting that God wanted to be glorified, Esther went that week to Faith Alive and approached Dr. Chris.

"The Lord has asked me to volunteer here," she said boldly, "and I want to go to the counseling unit. I want to reach out to people who are HIV-positive."

Dr. Chris looked at her quizzically, so she showed him her ID card.

"Oh, you are a pastor," he said, looking at her with the respect he offered people of God. With a discerning spirit and not one to stand in the way of God's plan for other people, he introduced her to the head counselor.

In March 2003, Pastor Esther began counseling thousands of people before and after their HIV tests. She fearlessly became an active participant at the weekly HIV-positive support group that she was once too ashamed to attend. The sewing and knitting school students began learning from her daily discipleship class lessons and looked to her as a role model.

She started referring pregnant women to Faith Alive's prenatal classes where nurses taught them how to prevent their unborn children from acquiring HIV.

A simple and inexpensive medicine, Nevirapine, she told them, given at the time of labor and delivery to the mother and to the infant after birth, drastically reduces the possibility of HIV infection.

Married couples began coming to Pastor Esther to learn that condoms could protect them from catching each other's strains of the virus. And she told women the best way to change their husband's hearts and habits—pray for them in the midst of intimacy.

Back at the "HIV and the Church" training in 2008, Pastor Esther posed a final question. She had already heard what these pastors and their wives thought about people with HIV. She wanted to talk about the great high priest.

"How do you think Jesus Christ would treat people with HIV if he were here today?"

Leaving just a moment for silence, she proceeded to preach about Jesus eating with the poor, befriending prostitutes, and touching lepers.

"Yes, even lepers," she said. "Jesus touched them. HIV is the modern-day leprosy, and we as the clergy need to lead the way. We need to model for others how to treat people with HIV in the same loving way that Jesus Christ did—with love, compassion, and forgiveness. Our churches need to be a refuge for suffering people."

"Now," she said, "let us hold the hand of the person sitting next to us and pray." Bowing her head, she started to pray aloud.

"In the mighty name of Jesus. Lord, we ask that you purify our hearts so that we can love others and ourselves unconditionally. Let us not ask people how they got HIV but ask how we can help. And let us approach your throne of grace with confidence, so that we may receive mercy and find grace to help us in our time of need. Amen."

● ● ●

Three years after that workshop, at Faith Alive in the presence of pastors and hundreds of friends and family, I saw Esther look directly into the eyes of her nervous yet smiling future husband.

We heard the pastor ask, "Is there anyone here who knows why this man and woman should not be joined in holy matrimony?"

The silence seemed deafening. Would anyone object to this now-openly HIV-positive bride marrying this groom? Someone had tried earlier that week to convince her groom to reject her because of her status. But he, also HIV-positive, remained undaunted by what he already knew and accepted. His unconditional love for whom he considered the most beautiful woman in the world was far stronger than people's fears and discrimination. Still, I saw the groom and his bride sigh with relief when nobody answered the pastor's question.

The wedding continued, and the couple vowed to love each other until death do them part. By God's grace, that will be many years away. In the meantime, they are living happily-ever-after.

The story of Chioma, Pastor Esther's former discipleship student at Faith Alive, also seems like a fairy tale. But both of these women know to thank God—not luck or fairy godmothers.

Cinderella Revisited

1996

Her voice swept through the field. Fourteen-year-old Chioma sang as she worked while her stepsiblings enjoyed a hearty meal of pounded yam and spicy egusi soup. Maybe there would be enough dinner remaining when Chioma finished her work and arrived home. Maybe her father would speak kind words to her today. Maybe today her stepmother would not hit her, causing another tear in her tattered skirt and spirit.

But instead of wondering about the future, she preferred to remember the past with her mommy.

"Beautiful girl," her mommy would say. "You are my princess. I took one look at you and knew that God existed."

She remembered following her mommy down the people-lined roads to the crowded market where produce sat on makeshift tables. Luxurious red tomatoes tasted like love. Mommy would pick up the vegetables, feel them for ripeness, and bargain for the best price. Before they reached home, Mommy would hand the best tomato to her only child to enjoy, one juicy bite at a time.

Chioma preferred to forget that her daddy had more than one wife at a time. Many of the village fathers did, increasing their chances for more children to do the cooking, cleaning, and farming before growing older and taking care of their parents and siblings. Chioma's daddy had two wives: his first, or senior one, and her mommy, the junior wife. The senior wife already had eight children and soon added another after Chioma entered this drama in 1982.

She had sensed, but was too innocent to name, how the senior wife treated Chioma's mommy. Years later, Chioma would better understand that a woman in any culture, monogamous or polygamous, did not like to share her husband with another woman—especially if the new wife was younger and prettier. The score did not bode well for Chioma's mommy. Senior wife: nine children. Junior wife: one.

When Chioma was seven years old, she heard that the senior wife tried unsuccessfully to poison Chioma's mommy. Feeling ill and fearing for her life, Chioma's mommy made the agonizing decision to leave behind her home and, even worse, her only beloved child. Chioma's daddy, typical of proud African men, took ownership of his family. With his military profession, he could and would hunt down any wayward children.

Before her mommy moved to another village to sell yams, she hugged Chioma.

"Be strong, my precious."

"But, Mommy," Chioma cried.

"Shh, shh," Mommy said. "Do not cry."

While Chioma's daddy allowed her to occasionally visit her mommy, their time together seemed far too short. Separation left a massive void of comfort.

The senior wife became Chioma's daily mother figure. Begrudgingly, she had to call her stepmother "Mama," much too endearing a name for someone who had no love for this inherited daughter.

Some things about daily life did not change, at least for a time. Chioma lived in the same hut, fetched water from the muddy stream, and hung clothes on the line to dry. She still walked through a path in the fields to her school where she learned to read and write. She played games with her stepsiblings, using tree seeds as game pieces and holes in the ground as their playing board.

While her stepsiblings continued to treat her as another family member, Mama did not. She manipulated her husband to believe lies about "this girl" who must have been a constant reminder of the junior wife.

"She is a wicked girl like her mother," Chioma heard Mama tell Daddy. "She is no good. Street boys will get her pregnant."

Chioma's daddy soon agreed. "You cannot do anything right, stupid girl," he said.

Their cruelty did not stop with words. Chioma's long, scarred legs told the story of beatings and accidents. While all the children did chores, Mama gave Chioma the heaviest loads of yam-like cassava to carry in a bucket on her head. Two times, the loads were too weighty. Her growing, gangly legs tripped and fell, spilling her cargo and ripping her legs on the rough, wooden blocks used to slow traffic. Instead of treating the wounds, Mama scolded her.

"Why are you so clumsy, stupid girl?"

Chioma hid her infected and permanently disfigured legs under long skirts, as if not seeing them denied the abuse.

Now fourteen years old and working in the cassava field, Chioma chose to focus on the good memories, the ones with her mommy. She hummed and sang tunes that Mommy taught her, songs that reassured her. Yes, love did exist.

When Chioma's hunger and aching back felt stronger than the approaching dusk, she started the slow walk home. She would have turned around and run if she knew what awaited her, what Mama had plotted for the next day when Chioma's daddy traveled.

After a sparse dinner that night, Chioma washed all the dishes. She bathed with cold water, trying to hide her blossoming figure from Mama's glare. Tonight, Mama's eyes seemed especially piercing. Maybe, Chioma thought, maybe Mama knows that I received a top score in my class, higher than her own children sometimes earned.

What Chioma did not learn in school, though, was that Mama had fetched a high bride price—money, fabrics, palm oil, chickens, and even a cow—from a thirty-one-year-old man in the city to marry Chioma, the beautiful virgin.

The next morning after Chioma did her chores and got ready to walk to school with her stepsiblings, Mama asked Chioma to stay. Curious but experienced enough to obey without questioning, Chioma waited. Mama is acting so strange, Chioma thought. Why is she asking me to go into the back closet? Wait, is she threatening me with a knife? No, this cannot be! Why, Mama, what have I done? A husband for me? No, I must struggle… everything is blurry.

For nearly two weeks, Chioma sat trapped in that windowless, locked room. There was no sanitary place to ease her bladder or bowels, and she only received scraps of food from Mama. Fortunately, one of Chioma's stepsisters had pity on Chioma's cries and sneaked her water and handfuls of leftover rice.

"Quick, take this before Mama sees."

Imprisoned alone in that stench-filled room, Chioma suffered until he arrived. He—her husband. No wedding ceremony, no celebrations, no love. Only her weakened body sold to this stranger. During the silent car ride into the city of Jos, she watched the landscape change. Cement homes and shanties interspersed with small storefronts, hospitals, and schools replaced mud huts and farmland. School, she thought, will I ever again go to school?

They finally stopped at a modest flat. He led her inside, locked the door, and kept the key. His police uniform and gun commanded a certain authority that she dared not challenge, making the lock unnecessary. She looked around and realized that at least she now had the freedom to roam around the flat, use a toilet, and prepare food.

But there was no freedom in the bedroom. After all, her husband paid quite a high dowry and expected certain things. As he hungrily eyed her developing curves, she felt a strong urge to kill him. However, she knew that would not release her from this new destiny.

After the initial trauma, Chioma began to see signs of her husband's kindness. Unlike Mama, he did not verbally abuse her. He bought her new clothes, provided enough food, and took her to the beauty salon.

One day he also took her to a doctor. He must have recognized what she did not. Nobody had explained to her that a nauseous feeling, tender breasts, and lack of menstrual flow were signs of pregnancy.

When she realized her situation, she cried. Now formal education will never be an option, she thought. My childhood is definitely over.

Totally dependent on him to provide for her and the baby growing in her womb, she stayed with her husband voluntarily. Strangely, this entrapment brought new freedom to leave and enter her home at will.

Her husband soon brought his pastor to visit and took Chioma to church. The pastor treated Chioma kindly and talked about God in a way she had never heard before. As a child, she had gone to church regularly but mostly heard about a vengeful and easily angered God. Now she heard about God's love, a love that she craved. Before long, the church became a welcome refuge, and God became the foundation for her new life.

God, I need you. I need your love, and I feel it here in this church.

Not long after, she gave birth to their first baby. Like many couples in this patriarchal Nigerian culture, they celebrated the glorious blessing of a male child. She had him in the hospital but did not receive any anesthesia for the excruciating pain. Taking one glimpse at the baby only fifteen years her junior, she prayed. *God, do you mean this came out of my body?*

She resigned herself to being a wife and mother. During the next few years, her husband continued his work and provided for his wife and son. Chioma dutifully prepared meals over the fire stove, swept the house with a broom of thin sticks, and hung the laundry on rope tied to the outside posts. Their son eventually started nursery school, and the next time Chioma's menstrual flow stopped, she understood why. After six years of marriage, their second son arrived.

Around this time, her husband's occasional cough got deeper and more regular. He lost his appetite and got sicker and slimmer by the day. When their boys were seven and two years old, her husband developed a stubborn bout of typhoid. Too proud to test for the underlying cause of his sickness, they both suspected

HIV but did not dare voice their fear of certain death and stigmatization.

Chioma faithfully filled the role of the good Nigerian wife—feeding, dressing, and cleaning her ill husband. She did not complain, even on the days when she also felt ill. After eight years together, she had developed some fondness for him. When he exhaled his last breath, she wept.

God, what will I do now? What about my boys? Help us, Lord.

Grieving, suspicious, and feeling increasingly sick a month after his death, she decided to test for HIV. The results confirmed her fears: full-blown AIDS. In 2004, only the wealthiest people could afford the lifesaving medications she needed. As a twenty-two-year-old widow, she believed that she would soon be buried beside her husband, leaving their cherished sons orphaned.

Her husband's mother, steeped in superstitions, accused Chioma's "bad spirits" of killing her grandchildren's father. Nigerian tradition gives the father's family ultimate rights to children and property, so Chioma's in-laws kept their son's flat and everything in it—including their grandsons—and kicked out Chioma.

Banished, weak, and desperate, Chioma prayed. *Please, God, take charge of my life. My boys need their real mother. And my heart cannot survive without them.*

She turned to her pastor, and he let her sleep on the church floor for a few days. Knowing that she needed medical help, he referred her to Faith Alive.

"I know about a place," he told her, "where I know the founding doctor. Let me write him a letter on your behalf."

Chioma willed herself to trek to the hospital and looked for a prominent doctor among the crowd. She saw a short man in a doctor's coat mingling and joking with patients, so she gave the letter to a tall staff person walking by to deliver to Dr. Chris. She felt shocked to see it handed to the ordinary-looking doctor.

Dr. Chris read the letter and approached her.

"You are welcome," he said as he guided her to an office. They sat down, and he said, "What is the problem?"

"I tested positive," Chioma said softly without looking into his eyes.

"We can help you. I will do another test to confirm. But I think there is something else, some other way that I can help you, right?"

Unsure how much to reveal but desperate, a few tears rolled down Chioma's sunken cheeks. She told him about losing her husband, her home, her possessions, and her sons.

"My dear," he said, touching her hand. "The best medicine right now is for you to be with your sons. Please, do not be scared. Let us see what God will do," he continued. "I think that later this week I can go with you to your in-laws' home. Yes, I will explain to them. We pray that they will listen to a doctor and have mercy on you."

True to his word, Dr. Chris, along with counselor Simon Odeh, took Chioma to her in-laws' home in an army barracks on the outskirts of Jos. When her in-laws saw her outside, they rushed the boys inside.

"Go away, you murderer," her mother-in-law spewed. "We don't want your sickness."

Dr. Chris slowly approached Chioma's father-in-law whose body blocked the door. "Sir," he said, "my name is Dr. Christian Isichei from Faith Alive."

"Why are you here?" her father-in-law bellowed.

"Sir, do you love God? I am here to ask you to take pity on your daughter-in-law." Then, getting down on his knees, Dr. Chris said, "I beg of you."

Their stubborn hearts refused. Dr. Chris, Simon, and Chioma had to return to Faith Alive empty-handed.

With no place to live and no way to provide for herself, Dr. Chris rented a flat for the defeated yet grateful Chioma. The tiny, pink flat in Faith Alive's transitional housing felt spacious to her with two rooms divided by a large piece of fabric hanging from the ceiling.

Dr. Chris's generosity did not end there. He invited Chioma to join a skills-acquisition class offered free-of-charge by Faith Alive. She chose to join the sewing class with a dozen other women, about half of them HIV-positive. Some of them were also single mothers who brought their babies either tied to their backs with colorful fabric or crawling on the cement floor between the foot-pedaled sewing machines.

Chioma's physical health gradually improved with the unconditional care and helpful learning she received at Faith Alive. All the knitting and sewing students and their small children squeezed into a little back room to start each morning with an hour-long discipleship class. Pastor Esther, a no-nonsense teacher, required them to memorize and recite Bible verses.

Pastor Esther invited Chioma to attend Faith Alive's HIV-positive weekly support group. She met dozens of others living positively with the virus who worked, thrived, and even made plans for the future. They learned about HIV prevention, healthy habits, money management, and other applicable topics.

Is it true that I might not die from AIDS, God, at least not now? Maybe not, but I might die from missing my boys.

She spent her days learning in class and nights praying on her tear-stained pillow. She wrestled between honoring tribal law and risking everything to be with her sons. Strong maternal instincts prevailed. She started to save and scrimp enough money from her sewn items to use for transport back to her in-laws' home.

About six months after moving into transitional housing, Chioma had tucked away just enough to travel the dusty roads. She tossed and turned in bed that night. The next morning, anticipating her in-laws' protests, she packed a traditional gift of fabric to offer them.

Probably because Chioma looked healthier, her in-laws this time allowed her to stay for a short visit. She bravely approached them a few days later.

"Please," she said with a combination of humility and boldness. "May I please take my boys to live with me?"

They refused, saying, "The boys will stay here and work hard for us."

Fearful that their mother might leave without them again, her sons stayed next to Chioma's side. This only fueled her courage to complete her mission. She held her boys' hands and silently prayed. *God, show us the way.*

The next day, her father-in-law left for work. A few hours later, her mother-in-law went to the market. Seeing an opportunity, Chioma quickly grabbed her sons. She rushed to find a motorbike taxi, and all three squeezed aboard. With fierce determination, they sped to safety.

They were back at Faith Alive's transitional housing before her in-laws must have realized what happened. She heard later that her father in-law had frantically started his own journey to Faith Alive to retrieve his grandsons. On the way, he had an accident on the bumpy roads and broke a leg. Believing the accident was a strong sign to leave his grandsons alone, he returned to his village.

At Faith Alive, the test results showed both Chioma's sons to be HIV-negative. The boys would inherit their parents' genes but not acquire their virus.

As Chioma thanked God, another young woman sharing their flat in transitional housing struggled with her baby daughter's HIV-positive symptoms. Despite Faith Alive's best efforts, the baby's chronic fever worsened, and she eventually died.

Oh, God, I do not know why babies die. But I choose to believe that you are a good God with great love. May your love sustain us.

Dr. Chris soon met a pregnant sixteen-year-old girl who, rejected by her parents, needed the transitional housing space. Chioma and her boys needed to move. Dr. Chris helped them rent a room in a different compound where she and her boys shared a double-sized mattress on the floor. No mosquito net hung overhead yet, but Faith Alive provided malaria treatments when needed.

That spring, Chioma joined the other sewing school graduates. Each received a brand new, foot-pedaled sewing machine from Mennonite Central Committee through Faith Alive to start their own businesses. Like many of the young women, she used her machine at home to make and sell clothes; her income went toward rent and food.

Hungry to learn more, Chioma spent years studying in the evenings by candlelight. By 2011, she passed the equivalent of a high school diploma and hoped to study business. Without a husband to rely on, she invested time and energy in her own earning potential with hopes for university admission someday.

She does not know how she might pay full school costs, but that does not stop her—like many Nigerians—from pursing her education one day, one semester at a time.

Her boys' school fees sapped her income. She appreciated Faith Alive's Angel Scholarship Program that helped with one of her son's school costs. As a single parent, she struggled to keep them on track with homework and hired a tutor when she had enough money.

●　●　●

Chioma told me that she considers Dr. Chris a father to her and her boys, God the father in flesh. She still turns to Dr. Chris, but only when she is desperate. She realizes that many people come to him because he knows how to tackle problems successfully.

Sometimes she takes her boys to see her biological mother who had remarried and has three more children. Travel is expensive, so the visits are not as often as Chioma and her sons would like. When together, Chioma stays at her mother's side cooking, cleaning, and washing clothes to make up for the years of separation.

Though her father died a few years ago, Chioma still has to see her stepmother occasionally at important gatherings like weddings and funerals. Chioma feels safe enough now to take the boys back to visit their paternal grandparents at Christmas. Nobody apologizes to her, but she chooses to forgive them. When she holds a grudge, she told me that she feels guilty talking with God. When she forgives, she feels better about herself and can worship God freely.

Her mother-in-law fell sick once and came to Chioma for help at Faith Alive. The staff graciously received her relative, ending ill feelings.

Unlike a fairy tale princess, Chioma does not have a magical godmother who is a plump, older, white woman in a sparkling evening gown waving a magic wand. Instead, she has a small, black man in a white doctor's coat and a faithful God. While her life is much improved, she is not living an unrealistic happily-ever-after. Her life has ups and downs. But she focuses on the ups, like sunshine when it reappears after a long, stormy darkness.

And her Prince Charming? Because of her beauty, many men ask her out, but she is wise enough to know what they really want. She has never experienced romantic love and longs for a husband who appreciates her character traits. I once jokingly suggested that she find a wonderful, blind man. She just cackled her loud, hearty laugh and said, "I don't have time to take care of my boys *and* a blind man!"

Maybe not, but with her sense of humor, intelligence, and faith, she is finding her voice and singing God's praises. Even deadly religious crises, including the one that nearly took her coworker's life, cannot dim her joy.

Nurse with a Purse

You have heard that it was said, 'Love your neighbor and hate your enemy.' But I tell you, love your enemies and pray for those who persecute you, that you may be children of your father in heaven.

Matthew 5:43–45a

August 2011

Nurse Caroline lifted her long, athletic legs off the motorcycle taxi that delivered her to work that morning. She paid the driver while protecting her black purse tightly against her side. The shiny bag bulged as if it held a baby. She poised her elbow, ready to bat away anyone who might try to steal it.

As she entered the Faith Alive Hospital, the young nurse smiled at both Christian and Muslim patients sitting on rows of wobbly benches.

"Inakwana?" she asked some coworkers to find out if they had slept well.

"Lafiya," they replied automatically.

She neared the small, locked office she shared with a doctor and treatment support specialist. Her hand delved into her purse, fingered around the deep recesses, and emerged with a key. She unlocked the door, entered, and closed it behind her. Putting the key in her pocket, she saw the familiar old box in the corner, shielded by the wooden desk. She carefully lifted the stack of tattered papers inside and buried her purse.

Now she was free to think about the day's patients. Hopefully, she thought, little Tina and Matta's mother would bring them today. Caroline and Julie, the nutritionist, wanted to see if the girls were still gaining weight. Just four weeks ago, their frail three- and five-year-old bodies had wasted to skin and bones. With FANOL Paste, the vitamin-enriched peanut butter that Julie had made and given them, the sisters were already showing remarkable improvement.

Dear God, please take care of them. If I were blessed enough to be their mother, I would feed them well. You know that I am ready to be a mother and a wife.

Caroline heard a knock at her door reminding her to lead the morning devotion for all staff and patients. Ah, she had nearly forgotten. Leaving her office, she locked the door behind her and hurried toward the waiting room packed with a sea of people. They had to look nearly as high as the top of the door to see Caroline's bright eyes and infectious smile. At six feet two inches, she towered above almost everyone.

She began to sing words of thanks to God, "Sai dai da kalmar godiya." She raised her arms freely, encouraging those well enough to stand. People too sick and frail stayed seated, leaning against someone else or on one of the concrete columns. Most people raised their voices and clapped to the familiar, irregular rhythm.

The group swayed and continued to sing well-known praise songs as if their energy powered the hospital's main generator. It, like an overworked actor, sometimes refused to perform. But this day the generator, and they, roared to life. Soon someone handed Caroline a microphone. Now magnified, the joyous melodies drowned out the okada horns and children playing in the schoolyard across the street.

After ten minutes, Caroline invited the crowd to sit. Pointing to the handwritten sign behind her, "Understanding the Times," she began talking about Faith Alive's spiritual theme for the month based on 1 Chronicles 12. She did not name the ongoing political and socio-economic divisions fueled by religious separations so indelibly inked in Jos's identity, but talked generally about staying alert and being prepared in troubling times.

She knew this topic all too well. Unrest was the reason she treasured her purse. But this was not the appropriate time or place to talk about that fateful day three years earlier.

On November 26, 2008, twenty-something Caroline had walked into her family's apartment after a long and fulfilling day tending to patients at Faith Alive. She greeted her two younger sisters, brother, and a cousin.

"Hello," they said to each other.

"How was work?" they asked Caroline.

"Fine," she said as usual and smiled. "Is Mama still out of town?"

"Yes," her brother said.

Caroline laid her small handbag on a bookshelf that held her nursing certificate and awards, photo of her late father, and collection of well-loved books. The smell of ginger, onions, and garlic wafted from the bright kitchen throughout the house. Her stomach growled in anticipation.

In the small bedroom that she shared with her sister, Grace, Caroline took off her necklace. She replaced her snug work clothes with a loose wrapper and a pair of well-worn slippers. Humming, she scuffled back into the kitchen.

"Where are the children?" she asked, referring to the neighbor kids who normally greeted her outside each evening. Often they raced each other for the honor of carrying Caroline's purse.

"Me, me!" the six of them would project over each other's voices.

If one of them carried their youngest sibling, that baby would stretch his arms out to Caroline. He did not vie for her purse, but for the security of her strong arms and comfort of her broad smile below smooth, high cheekbones.

"We have not seen them yet," Caroline's cousin Abeje said. "Will you go and knock on their door? It will soon be time to swallow the chop. I made enough of their favorite pounded yam for us to take to them."

Caroline walked outside past the compound gate to the next home. She noticed that the street seemed unusually quiet. She knocked on the Hassans' door.

No response.

Another knock and no answer. Caroline shouted out, "Hallo. Is anyone home?"

Only silence and darkness.

That is strange, she thought. They must be out, but they are usually home at this time of night. It is not a Muslim holiday, is it? No, Mr. Hassan is traveling, but Salamatu and the children should be home. Is someone ill?

Caroline returned home. If one of the Hassans was injured, perhaps her family could provide money again for treatment. They had done that for little Barak, the Hassan's oldest son.

After a little while, Caroline returned to her neighbors' door. Again, some knocks, and again, no response.

Another neighbor trekked by, so Caroline asked if he had seen the Hassans.

"We have not. If anyone would know where they are, it would be you," he said. "You are the ones who are always together with them."

As time increased, so did Caroline's worry. Something seemed strange, but she could not name it. Chatty little Muhammad always told her everything— even private details like when his parents argued or where they hid his father's sparse naira coins.

Later that night, without the children's regular singing, dancing, or doing homework with Caroline, she slipped under the mosquito net into bed beside Grace. Fortunately, Grace was thinner and half a head shorter than Caroline's tall, sturdily built frame so that both could fit comfortably. Caroline pulled the blanket up to her chin and prayed.

God, I do not know what is going on, but you do. Please keep the Hassans safe. Thank you that we are neighbors who watch over each other. In the mighty name of Jesus, Amen.

Caroline closed her eyes and did not open them until she heard the roosters crow. Rising with the sun as usual, she and Grace got out of bed and joined their family in the main room for morning devotions. After reading the Bible, singing, and praying, their brother left to get bread. Their most junior sister, Mary, filled buckets with well water. Caroline waited until Grace finished bathing and then walked toward the bathroom. She heard her handset ring.

"Hallo?" she answered.

"There is trouble in the streets. Fighting," she heard her brother say. "Please be careful."

"Where?"

"I am not sure," he said, "but it sounds bad."

"Thank you," she said before hanging up.

She had enough time to tell Grace and the others before they heard a commotion outside. They stepped out front just in time to see rocks raining over their compound wall. A handful of familiar young Muslim men, some she knew by name, stormed the compound's gate.

Wait, these are some of my neighbors! Oh, Lord, what is happening?

She heard screaming, or did it come from herself? She helplessly watched one boy that they knew throw gasoline on her family's apartment building. Another boy had a lighted torch. He swung back his arm, ready to launch.

"Please, please, no, no, no, do not do this. We are your neighbors!" pleaded Mary.

The other men and boys noticed Caroline's family and lurched toward them.

"Come on!" Caroline shouted to her sisters and cousin Abeje. But only Grace and Abeje were behind her. Headstrong Mary stood her ground, banking on her friendship with one of the boys.

Now in the throng of runners headed to a Christian neighborhood, Caroline raced as fast as her swift legs would carry her away from the chilling chaos. Smelling smoke, she looked back to see if Mary had joined them.

Instead, she saw some of the mob attacking other people, the slower ones, trying to escape. Sticks pounding. Knives cutting. Rocks thrown. Blood and screams of agony filled the streets as her legs carried her faster and farther.

With nothing but the clothes on their backs, Caroline, Grace, and Abeje darted between buildings and down dusty streets. Turning once more, Caroline saw an old man at the mercy of the angry mob. She saw blood oozing out of the man's head, streaming down the side of his ripped tunic. Feeling helpless and afraid for their own lives, she and her family could not stop to help.

She did not know if minutes or hours passed before she, Grace, and Abeje stopped and caught their breath. Her heart, pounding inside her chest, assured her that she still lived.

Looking around and seeing no mobsters, Caroline heard a group of women speaking Caroline's dialect—a Christian one.

"Please…help," Caroline managed to say to them. "An old man…is being beaten to…death. He needs to get…to the closest…hospital."

Oh, Lord, let them help this man. We must get to a safe place. Save us, show us where to go.

Looking around, Caroline recognized a friend's home. "This way," she motioned to Grace and Abeje.

When they arrived, Mrs. Gbong opened the door to the frantic trio. "Sannu, Grace, and…oh…what has happened?"

"We are fine," Grace said. "But Mary. Oh, Mary! She stayed to beg that please they not burn our house. Where is your handset? I hope it is not offed. Oh, dear Mama…praise God that she is traveling."

Not needing more of an explanation, Mrs. Gbong rushed to another room and returned with her phone. Grace dialed Mary's number. It rang, but nobody answered. She tried again with the same result.

"Try Brother," Caroline suggested, as they huddled around the phone.

"Hallo?" Grace said when their brother answered. "Fine…yes, Caroline and Abeje, too…the Gbongs… Mary stayed….oh *thank God*! Thank you, Jesus! Yes… stay safe." Caroline, Abeje, and Mrs. Gbong's tense faces burst into smiles as they raised their clasped hands to heaven.

Grace hung up and explained that their brother had rushed home in time to see Mary running away. Another friend had soon called him to say that Mary was safe with her. Also, he said that police raced to the scene to help.

Assured of Mary and their brother's safety, Caroline remembered the bleeding man.

God, do you want us to help him? Is he alive?

"Mrs. Gbong," Caroline said. "Grace and I should go to the hospital near here."

"Wait," Mrs. Gbong said. "I will send my oldest, Marcus, with you for protection."

"Thank you. That is a good idea."

The three arrived at the hospital gate just in time to see two policemen carrying the old man away from the front door.

"What is happening?" Grace asked the policemen.

"Nobody is here to help," he said. "The doors are locked."

Knowing that the hospital staff probably had not made it to work yet through the violence-infested streets, Caroline started to say, "I am a nurse." But the words did not come. She looked down at her shaking hands and knew that they, as well as her emotional state, were not steady. Everything rocked—her hands, her head, her world.

Defeated, the sisters and Marcus returned to the Gbongs' home. It provided a temporary haven that day while they waited, shell-shocked, for Mary and their brother. They alternated between crying, staring blankly, and praying. They soon learned that their home and all their possessions had completely burned in the fire.

"Kai!" their brother said in disgust after he arrived. "Jos is supposed to be the home of peace and tourism. But these days there is so much unrest. Why are innocent Christians being targeted again? Such senseless violence."

As this new personal reality started to sink in, Caroline turned to them and asked, "You do not think, do you…is it possible that the Hassans knew about this? Surely they would have warned us, at least. Remember how Mr. Hassan protected our home when Muslims attacked in 2001? Maybe that is why they were not home, because they did not know what to do. But I thought they were our family."

Caroline soon learned that many Muslims in Jos were warned ahead of time about the planned attacks. She did not want to see the Hassans to confirm if they knew ahead of time; their desertion that night spoke volumes. The fact that the Hasssans' home also burned or that Mr. Hassan had suffered a stroke after learning about his own losses was not much consolation.

The Gbongs offered to house Caroline's family, but there were no spare beds and little floor space.

When Dr. Chris learned about her plight, he rushed to her.

"I am sorry. I am sorry," he told her.

His genuine concern gave Caroline freedom to be vulnerable. She let a tear slide down her cheek, something she normally allowed only behind closed doors.

"Angel," he said, using his term of endearment for all his nurses, "do you remember Samson in the Bible?"

"Yes, I do. I do," she said, nodding slightly.

"Do you remember that all his strength came through his long hair?"

Once again, Caroline nodded.

"Do you remember that his wife deceived him and sold that secret information to his enemies? Because of this, they shaved Samson's hair, gouged his eyes, and put him in prison."

She listened intently, still unclear what relevance this had to her situation. It certainly did not encourage her.

Dr. Chris said, "The Book of Judges says that his hair grew again."

Dr. Chris put his hand on Caroline's arm. "It is like you don't have hair now," he said, looking up into her brown eyes, "but it will grow again."

Dr. Chris and the Faith Alive family offered her a temporary bed at the guesthouse. She accepted, grateful that her employer and coworkers treated her like extended family. They provided for her basic immediate needs, even though it was difficult to find clothing long enough for Caroline's tall body.

Caroline's heartbeat rose as the sun went down each night. Her head filled with visions of the fresh corpses she had seen, the fires, the fleeing. Sleep provided no rest from the nightmare she had experienced. The horrific images, smells, and sounds filled her thoughts.

When Caroline's family finally found a permanent home in a Christian area, Dr. Chris gave her money to replace some essential furniture. New beds and dressers sat against walls that should have displayed numerous family photos.

Caroline also bought a new purse. A large, black, shiny one—big enough to cradle valuables like her identity card, naira, and keys. Much like a child's security blanket, it rarely left her side. She had lost so much—photos of her father, diplomas, and a sense of safety. If she ever had to escape quickly again, she wanted to grab her bag and run.

● ● ●

Like Samson, the hair on Caroline's head is growing, although she often wears a wig like many African women. Other times she wears a beautiful head wrap. Covering her head is much easier than expecting her brittle hair to perform with the hard well-water and blowing wind when she rides on the back of okadas.

In 2009, I gave her David Stoop's book *Forgiving the Unforgiveable*. We talked a week later.

Caroline said, "I saw them." I knew that she meant the Hassans. "They came into the hospital. I wanted to run, but I did not."

"What happened?"

"God gave me strength. I went up to them. I could tell that the children wanted to reach out to me. Their eyes lit up when they saw me, but their mother kept them close. They are innocent. So I greeted them and took their medical files to their doctor."

Caroline paused.

"Then I had to leave the hospital. I had to get some air. That is all I can do for now, but it is a start. The book talked about loving our enemies and forgiving others as we would have them forgive us. Honestly, it helped a lot. I have not had a nightmare since I read it."

More than three years after that horrific morning, Caroline still carries her big purse everywhere. She will not tell anyone exactly what is in it, except that it holds her important documents. But it does not hold the intangible—her good health, loving family, compassionate friends, loyal employer, hard-earned education, and secure faith in Jesus Christ.

Over time, she has developed a sense of humor about her purse. In 2010, she told me that she had travelled for a children's health care conference. She had settled into an airplane seat for the ride to Kenya. After fastening her seatbelt, she clutched her bag in her lap before takeoff.

"Ma'am," the flight attendant told her, "your bag needs to go under the seat in front of you or in an overhead bin."

"I will hold it," Caroline said.

"It is an airline regulation," the attendant said firmly while reaching down to take the purse.

As soon as the attendant's hand touched it, Caroline instinctively gripped it like a child protecting her security blanket from a monster before bedtime.

Perhaps realizing she needed to take a different tactic, the flight attendant smiled and gently said, "Trust me. It will be right at your feet where you can reach it once we are in the air."

Remembering from other flights about this routine requirement, Caroline reluctantly stuffed her bulging purse under the seat. But she secured the bag's strap around her right foot.

She soon realized that carrying hatred against her neighbors became too heavy a burden. With God's help, Caroline is working on loving the Hassans. The process has not been easy or immediate. The pain remains. For her, like many people, forgiveness is a journey, one that does not allow her to forget the pain or wait for the Hassans to apologize.

As she prays for them, her heart lightens. Maybe one day her purse will, too. She has begun to enjoy befriending Muslims, but feels most certain that she would never marry one like her coworker Helen had.

Pills under the Pillow

You are the God who performs miracles; you display your power among the peoples.

Psalm 77:14

2002

Dr. Chris took one look at the semi-conscious woman rushed into the hospital on a young man's back and knew that it would take God's intervention for her to live. He had seen too many people this close to death succumb to the end. He tired of writing death certificates almost daily, given that ARVs for HIV-positive patients at that time were a luxury. But worry did not overcome him. He worked for a powerful God.

"Here now," he said to the young man while pointing to an examination table in a room next to the entryway. Escorting them into the room, Dr. Chris said, "Let us lay her here. Gently now."

The woman's shriveled, near-skeletal body flopped like a ragdoll onto the black vinyl tabletop supported by upturned stools. She gasped for her next breath but seemed too weak to moan.

"Is this your mother?" Dr. Chris asked the young man who turned to look at the older woman and man now entering the hospital door.

"Doctor," the older woman said, pausing for a breath after hurrying inside from a taxi. "I am his mother. And hers. My daughter, Helen," she said, pointing to the patient. "She is age thirty-one. Please, can you do anything to help her?"

"By God's grace," Dr. Chris replied. Realizing that his patient's illness had weathered her far beyond her years, he asked, "What is the problem?"

The mother wrung her hands and said, "She is HIV-positive. For a few years she has taken her HIV medicine, but I am a widow and…and our money is exhausted. Worse still, we have been told for the past three months that the medicine is not even available." What she did not say, could not will herself to speak, was that another of her adult children had died a few years earlier from AIDS-related tuberculosis.

"Do not worry," Dr. Chris said, looking first at the mother and then at the rest of the family. "Everything we do here is for free. Let us see what God will do." Seeing the mother frown as if in disbelief, he said, "We do not ask a fee."

Based on her experiences with other Nigerian doctors and hospitals where patients are not treated or released until payment, the mother did not believe

Dr. Chris. She turned to her elder brother for help. He reached into his wallet, brought out the little naira he had, and handed it to Dr. Chris.

"No, no, no," Dr. Chris said, realizing the need to repeat himself. "You do not need to pay. First, we will see what we can do for your daughter, but here we do not charge any money. If you want to donate, that is fine."

Knowing that the patient needed immediate attention, Dr. Chris quickly bent down to check her vital signs. "Helen," he said as he bent down toward her ear, "I am going to take good care of you. You are just going to feel a little pinch." Helen did not flinch as he inserted a needle into one of her veins. After first withdrawing a blood sample into a vial and labeling it, he reached into the wall cabinet and got an IV bag. He hung it from a lopsided pole and connected Helen to this fortified liquid.

"Your daughter's condition is very serious," he told Helen's mother. "I will take her blood sample to the lab to help me know how best to treat her." Seeing no scarf on her head, he asked the mother, "Are you a Christian?"

"I am," she said, nodding.

"Please pray for your daughter."

She nodded but then realized that he wanted her to pray right now, together. So she closed her eyes and said firmly, "In the mighty name of Jesus, heal my daughter. We know that you are the God of miracles, and we plead with you to do one now and spare her life. Forgive us for any way that we have offended you, and bring your spirit's healing power to her now. In Jesus' name we have prayed. Amen!"

"Amen," Dr. Chris and the others echoed. Then he said, "God hears his children's prayers." He leaned toward the mother and placed his hand on her arm. "Please, Mama, do not worry. Pray without ceasing."

As he left the room with the sample, Helen's mother said, "God bless you."

Within three or four hours, Helen's heavy eyelids strained to open. She drifted in and out of consciousness, hearing her mother sing and pray for her. "In the name of Jesus Christ, Holy Father, the Alpha and the Omega, bring my daughter back to life. Protect her from anything evil and give her long life for her two daughters. Oh, God, I ask this in the name of Jesus."

Helen's mind wandered from sleep to dreams to reality back to dreams again in no coherent order.

Is this my husband here...has he forgiven me for converting back to Christianity, or is he still angry at me for not being a Muslim...get out of my house, he says, and take these daughters. They are not mine any longer....

Helen's eyes opened, but her husband was not there. Only her faithful mother—a widow—sat by Helen's bedside while Helen's children stayed with their aunt.

Jehovah, you are the one true God, Jehovah...mama, mama, my daughters say...come and play with me...more drip...she is getting better. Are these voices in my head or are they real...tired...so tired...

Days passed with peaks of hope when Helen opened her eyes and talked and also valleys of slow, raspy, semiconscious breaths. Dr. Chris knew that her CD4 count, the measure of what he called a body's natural soldiers to fight infection, dipped to thirty-seven. A healthy person's army had over 500; anything below 200 in someone with HIV indicated clinical AIDS. Helen's count put her in the immediate danger zone.

Her mother and a nurse tried to cajole Helen to take food that her mother brought. Because Nigerian hospitals do not usually feed patients, Helen's mother brought either rice or bread daily. When Dr. Chris heard that Helen still refused to eat well during the first week, he came to her bedside.

"Please, Helen," he said, bending down to feel her cheek, "what is your favorite food?

Helen shrugged lethargically and said nothing.

"I have an excellent cook at home," he said after about ten seconds. He knew what most Nigerians loved to eat. "She makes delicious pounded yam—good enough for a king!"

Helen managed a small smile.

"Yes, I will get some pounded yam for you, my princess!"

Early the next morning, he brought her a Sprite and insulated container filled with steaming yam. "Excellent!" he said as she reached for it. He helped raise her body to a slight sitting position propped by a pillow against the wall. "Yes, chop—eat," he said. "Oh, that is so good! And drink now."

Helen's mother marveled at this doctor who took such a personal interest in Helen. She waited until Dr. Chris left the room and said to her daughter, "Oh, Jesus, what kind of place is this? Who is this man who gives you not just medicine but is feeding you, too? Is this real?"

Helen nodded but concentrated on swallowing. She needed to retrain her body to do its simple work of eating, drinking, sitting, and walking. She faced a long uphill climb on this journey back to life.

She needed to exercise her atrophied muscles. One day she sat upright on her own and hung her legs over the bed. A nurse, seeing this, came to Helen's side, took her arms, and steadied her to stand on the gray concrete floor. It took nearly a month before Helen gained enough weight and strength to walk to the end of the room.

Dr. Chris monitored Helen's slow but steady recovery. Believing that people recover fastest in their own environments and needing the space for other patients, Dr. Chris released Helen to her mother's house and care. Four weeks after Helen had been too weak to walk through the gate, she stepped carefully out of the hospital.

Her mother, by her side, carried a month's worth of Helen's ARVs in her purse. She guarded it as if it were lined with diamonds. She did not know that years later, ARVs would come from the United States government's PEPFAR program for international AIDS relief. In the meantime, ARVs remained a rare luxury in Nigeria.

"But I have no money to pay," Helen's mother had told Dr. Chris that morning when she saw the medicine. "And the cost of her to stay here. We can only pay you a little bit at a time."

"Ah, Mama Helen," he said affectionately, using the term for someone else's mother. "I told you, now. We give God the glory. Do you remember the American who visited Helen last week? She gave me these medications."

"Lord Almighty!" Helen's mother shouted as Helen's jaw dropped.

"Yes, please take," he said as he pushed the medicine into her hands. "Go now, and make sure that she takes them at the same time every morning and every evening." Then he turned to Helen and said, "Keep coming to your appointments here. When you are stronger, we can talk about our knitting school. You can learn how to make beautiful things—things fine enough to sell to a queen!"

Overcome by this doctor's compassionate generosity, Helen's mother dropped to her knees. She raised her hands toward heaven and said, "Oh, Jesus, you are great!" Still kneeling, she reached up to the doctor standing beside her and said, "May God richly reward you and your family. I can never repay you."

Once home, Helen's mother carefully searched the house for a place to hide the drugs—a triple cocktail of healing, health, and hope. Scurrying from room to room, she saw her lumpy, tear-stained pillow. She lifted it and placed the pills underneath. Yes, this mother would sleep on them at night, protecting them if any noise or movement threatened her daughter's health.

Helen continued to heal and add weight. A few months later, her children moved back home. Feeling stronger every day and regaining her hearty laugh, she soon enrolled in Faith Alive's knitting school. As he did with all the students, Dr. Chris paid her a token amount for transport fees to and from class and also for some feeding. Helen learned to knit well but didn't stay through graduation because he invited her to join the staff as a treatment support specialist.

"Helen, my dear," Dr. Chris said, "we need you to work in a team with a doctor and nurse. We need someone who is positive in status and attitude to relate to the patients on a more personal level as well as assist the medical team with whatever they need—cleaning, arranging folders, weighing patients, and encouraging them." He looked at Helen's broad smile and knew that she would accept even before he told her that she would earn a salary.

"Of course," she said. "I will do whatever you want me to do. You saved my life."

Dr. Chris shook his head and said, "God saved your life. We gave you medicine that helped assist, but it is only God that brings healing. He is the miracle-giver. You are a testimony to his faithfulness, and we give him all the thanks and glory."

Helen nodded in agreement and said, "You have spoken the truth. Yes, God is my heavenly Father. But you," she said, "you are my earthly daddy."

● ● ●

When I saw Helen in 2011, she looked healthy—plump actually—and still took modified first-line drugs for her HIV treatment. Dr. Chris was amazed that her body did not develop resistance that commonly occurs during lapses in taking the medicine. If resistance happens, patients need to start much more expensive second-line drugs that are still a luxury in developing countries.

The nonprofit Tearfund had hired Helen as a spokeswoman at HIV-awareness trainings where she talks openly about her status and experience coming back to life. A poster features her before-and-after photos. Next to her pictures on the poster, the tagline reads, "God cares, and so do we at Faith Alive."

Her Muslim husband, the one who absolved himself of all family responsibilities after her conversion to Christianity, contacted Helen for help. Out of money and failing on his first-line of ARVs, Helen took pity on him and brought him to her favorite doctor. Even though their marriage had officially ended, she still referred to him as her husband.

"Daddy," she said to Dr. Chris, "this is my husband."

Feeling ashamed for infecting his wife and leaving her near-death, he hung his head. Yes, Dr. Chris knew their story. About the same time that their marriage began disintegrating due to his womanizing, she had felt increasingly uncomfortable with the Muslim faith. She went to church with a friend and heard the pastor say that everyone had to make a choice for or against Jesus Christ. She felt compelled to return to her Christian roots and knew that staying with her husband would not help.

Dr. Chris welcomed Helen's husband with a smile. "You are welcome here, sir," Dr. Chris said.

Helen's husband started to apologize to Dr. Chris, the man who had taken over his responsibilities providing medicine and a job for his wife as well as school fees for his daughters.

Dr. Chris listened and said, "Do not worry, now. You are welcome here."

Then, reciting from the Dedication Declaration he had written and recited with his staff at each weekly meeting, he said, "Your past has been forgiven, your future is secure, and God has a purpose for your life."

Amazed, Helen's husband slowly mirrored part of the smile on this doctor's face.

"Let us see what God will do," Dr. Chris said. "People enter this place, some with legs too weak to support them. By God's miracles, many leave stronger, walking out toward health and a future."

Some also stay, hired by Dr. Chris to share their newfound strength with others. That is true of other staff I know, including Chede.

Righteous Reversal

The LORD says… 'Sit at the right hand until I
make your enemies a footstool for your feet.'

Psalm 110:1

2003

"I knew it!" the restaurant owner screamed at her sick worker. "You smell foul. Kai!" Her face twisted like a knotty tree, and her arms flailed toward him as if he had just released a swarm of deadly mosquitoes. "Out before we are all sick and die! Never you come back. Never! Worthless man, killing my business."

Chede shamefully bowed his head to avoid his boss's physical slings. But her verbal ones had already taken up residence in his head and heart. He shuffled out the doorway, leaving behind his job, his pride, and his only source of income to feed his wife and children.

Walking slowly down the dirt road, he avoided eye contact with everyone, convinced that they all knew where his ambling life of drinking and smoking had led him. *Oh, God, why did I tell her my status? She now knows that I am nothing more than manure, the dirty, worthless smell that I cannot control. I might as well just die now before AIDS kills me. Ayyyyii, but who will feed my family? Jesus Christ, what next am I to do?*

As his shame turned to indignation—a more familiar emotion—Chede summoned a motorbike to take him to the Faith Alive Hospital. It was the same place his boss had forced him to go last week to get tested for HIV, the virus that she suspected as the cause of his red eyes and frequent need to use the toilet. The hospital where Dr. Chris, when counseling Chede after receiving a positive status a few days later because results were not immediate in 2003, advised him to be honest with his boss.

"I will show him how well that worked," Chede said to himself as he breathed the bike's excess black fumes. "Be honest. Hmmmph!"

At the hospital, Chede pushed out his chin and marched toward the admissions' desk. He slapped his handcard onto the wooden sign-in table and announced that he needed to see Dr. Chris. Right now. Never mind that over a dozen people sat patiently in the queue ahead of him, some of them slouched against the wall.

"Is this an emergency?" the volunteer sitting behind the table asked.

"Yes," Chede said. Sensing that she wanted to know details, he added, "It is private. Between me and the doctor."

Moved by his determination and sense of urgency, the volunteer walked to a closed door, knocked, and entered another room. A few minutes later, she came out with a patient and motioned for Chede, still standing, to enter.

He shot past the door. But as soon as he saw Dr. Chris's earnest eyes looking directly at him, Chede's angry facade began to melt.

"What is the problem?" Dr. Chris asked as Chede sank into the plastic chair next to the doctor's small, metal desk.

Chede explained his unsuccessful confession and desperate outlook.

"Oh," Dr. Chris said as he nodded his head to encourage Chede to talk.

After a few more minutes, Chede stopped talking and sighed.

Dr. Chris turned his head from left to right and back again, as if shaking off the stigma and shame and said, "Please do not worry. Our God is faithful, and he will make a way out for us."

But Chede did not hear the "us," did not yet realize that this doctor doing God's work would sacrifice his own money to help. Chede only hung his head and held back the waterfall of tears that wanted to gush past his eyes.

"Doctor," Chede's voice barely eked out loud enough for either of them to hear. "I am no longer living in this world. I will go hang myself and die."

"No," Dr. Chris said adamantly. "There is life after testing positive. You have met Ruth, yes?"

Chede nodded affirmatively.

"You may not know, however, that she is HIV-positive."

Chede squinted his eyes to see this new reality.

"Yes," Dr. Chris said. "She is open to talk with you. She is proof that people can live positively. HIV stands for "Hope Is Vital." God has a plan for your life."

Then, valuing human lives more than finances, Dr. Chris reached into his pocket, took out his skinny, weathered wallet, and asked, "How much did you earn at the restaurant?"

Chede answered hesitantly, "Three thousand naira a month, sir."

"Here," Dr. Chris said as he took 1,500 naira out of his wallet and put it on the table for his desperate patient to accept or reject. "Here is half of your first month's pay at Faith Alive."

Jutting his left ear forward to hear better, Chede asked, "Excuse me?"

"Yes," Dr. Chris said. "I want you to work here at Faith Alive. And I will pay you the same amount that you earned at the restaurant."

"But…" Chede asked, "what do you need me to do?"

"We need someone to help others, like Ruth who understands what it is like to be HIV-positive. First, though, your lifestyle will need to change," he said, intuiting correctly that beer had stained Chede's dirty, white shirt.

Chede looked at Dr. Chris, then the money, and then the doctor before he saw that this offer was real— not one of the hallucinations or bad dreams he had been having lately, but honest to goodness reality.

Oh, thank you, Jesus. Who is this doctor who knows my darkness yet wants me to work for him and even pays me before I have done any work? Can this be real?

Chede took the offer and the money and came back the next day to start in the maintenance department. He came back the next day, and the next year, and a few years after that until the day he saw his former restaurant boss again.

His health had improved. He had stopped smoking and drinking and got serious about going to church and reading his Bible. Someone from the United States financed his lifesaving ARVs until PEPFAR funds were available at Faith Alive. His renewed appetite fueled his body's growth as he regularly took his drugs. A few years later, Dr. Chris promoted Chede to the counseling department.

On a sunny day in 2011, Chede sat behind a desk in his Faith Alive office with Sarah, a young HIV-positive woman whose doctor referred her to adherence counseling before commencing her ARV drug regimen.

"See, you do not joke with your drugs," Chede told Sarah as he looked at her medical file and saw her low CD4 count number.

Sarah looked a bit too casual for Chede, so he admonished, "This is serious. It is the only way for you to live. See, if you do not take your drugs or even multivitamins regularly, your body develops a resistance. And then your drugs will not work."

Still not convinced that Sarah understood the severity of the situation, he added, "You see me now. I know what I am talking about. If you do not take your drugs every morning and every evening, you will die. Do you want to die?"

She looked at him like he had asked a stupid question and said, "No, of course not."

"Then remember to take what your doctor will give you. What time do you say your prayers every morning?"

"Six-thirty."

"What do you do at six-thirty in the evening?"

"I prepare food with my sisters."

"Okay then," Chede said. "It will be easy. Take your drugs every morning before prayers and every evening while the rice is cooking. Soon it will be natural."

But Sarah did not hear his last words because her handset rang. She quickly fetched it from her purse and offed it.

"Ah," Chede said, remembering another tactic. "You have a handset. That is very good. It should have an alarm. You can set your phone to beep at six-thirty every morning and evening."

"Yes," she said at the mention of her phone, the link now to more than her social life. "I can do that. It is a good idea."

"It is so good that you must do it right now. Yes," he said, motioning to her handset, "set it right now."

He watched as Sarah pressed a few digits and waited until he was convinced that her alarm functioned correctly.

"Well done," he said. "Now come back in one month and let me know how you are doing."

A few minutes after Sarah left his office, Dr. Chris walked in with a woman who looked eerily familiar.

"See Chede here," Dr. Chris told her. "We are so proud of his work. He is a very hard worker, and he can help you."

Seeing his current boss standing next to his former one, like the light shining on darkness, Chede sat up straight and looked directly into the woman's eyes.

"Good afternoon," Chede said confidently. The gray in her formerly black hair reminded him that it had been years since their last encounter.

"Ah…um…yes…I see that you are doing well," she said, recognizing her former employee. She seemed to try not to reveal shock that he was still alive, let alone now important enough to have an office.

Sensing the tension that he had hoped for, Dr. Chris reminded them of his presence by saying, "Mrs. Onyevil has brought one of her employees here to be tested for HIV, much like she did with you many years ago. Would you please help them?" Then Dr. Chris left the room to let God continue his act of justice.

Lord Jesus, oh, Lord almighty, can this be true? Am I, once the worthless goat begging at her feet, now the one with the food and she the one crying out for help? Oh, Jesus, help me glorify you even now when I want her to rot.

As if answering Chede's prayer instantly, restraint overtook his vengeful instincts, and he asked Mrs. Onyevil to bring the girl into his office.

"Sit down," Chede said to the girl as he motioned for her to sit in the only remaining chair that Mrs. Onyevil started to sit in. "What is your name?"

"Fatima," she said quietly, unaware of her role in this satisfying drama.

"Fatima," Chede asked, "what is the problem?"

She looked up at her boss for permission before turning to this counselor and saying, "I need to be tested for HIV."

He wanted to talk privately with this girl, but first wanted to address the broader problems. He, too, looked at his former boss, but not for permission.

"You," he said directly to Mrs. Onyevil, "Did you not bring in this your servant girl here to find out if she is killing you? And if she has HIV, you will disown her and leave her for dead as you did to me eight years ago?"

As if God could not hear her lies, Mrs. Onyevil said, "No, no, this is not what is happening. I just…I need to know if she has that virus so she can get help."

"Kai," Chede said, "this is selfish for you to bring in this girl so you can find out if she has it and if she has infected you. Then you will turn her away. That is called discrimination and you," he said while trying to control his rage, "you should not do that. Now go, let me talk to Fatima alone."

Mrs. Onyevil uncharacteristically submitted to her former employee, knowing that he controlled today's conversation. She got up, walked to the hallway, and waited on a bench.

Alone in the office with Fatima, Chede counseled her before, during, and after her blood test result, now revealed within a few minutes. It confirmed that she was, indeed, positive.

"Do not worry," he said, "God is faithful, and he will make a way out. But I do not trust that your boss will accept you. You would not be the first one she has rejected. Do you have family that can help?"

"No," Fatima said, dabbing her eyes with the small rag she carried. "That is why I have to live with and work for Mrs. Onyevil."

"Let me talk to Dr. Chris and see if you can stay in transitional housing here. And you can apply for our sewing or knitting skills-acquisition classes. All this is no fee. Really, there is a way out. Now," he told Fatima, "I must see Mrs. Onyevil. Would you please call her in on your way to wait in the hallway?"

"Yes, sir," Fatima said before she obediently summoned her boss.

Mrs. Onyevil walked into Chede's office after looking at Fatima's face and muttered disgustedly, "I knew it."

"Sit down," Chede said with an edge to his voice. "Yes, you now know her status," he affirmed in this culture without health privacy laws. "Are you satisfied?"

She sat down and whined, "She has probably infected me already. Kai!"

Resisting the urge to say that he hoped so, Chede took a clean form off the top of his stack of papers. He started writing her name.

"What is that for?" she asked.

"For your test," he said. Starting his routine pre-test counseling, he asked, "How will you feel if you are HIV-positive?"

"I…" she started to say and then stopped. She probably wanted to say that she would kill herself, or Fatima even, if that dirty girl infected her with such filth. Instead, she looked at her former employee living with HIV and reconsidered. "I would not like it," she said.

"Like it or not," Chede said with a sense of satisfaction, "you would have to accept it. People with HIV can live normal lives if they take their medications every day. As you can see, HIV is not a death sentence." Resisting the temptation to withhold Faith Alive's many services, he added, "At Faith Alive we offer free medications and doctor visits. We also have a weekly support group for people living positively with HIV."

Handing Mrs. Onyevil the paper, he told her to go to the hospital's lab for her test and come back with the paper.

While he waited for her to return, Chede called another of the many patients waiting in the hallway. It saddened him that he had to record "yes" for positive so many times in his daily record book.

An hour or two later, much longer than necessary, Chede called Mrs. Onyevil back into his office. She handed him the paper result, now stapled shut, and sat down. He watched her leg shake nervously as if to shoo away a pestering fly.

He used his yellowed teeth to slowly remove the staple and spit it on the floor. Then he slowly unfolded the paper, making sure to keep the stamped result from Mrs. Onyevil's sight. Looking at the paper, then at her, and then back to the paper, he had to be sure. He surprised himself by feeling a wave of sadness when he had expected the joy of justice.

She waited for him to speak.

"You are HIV-positive," Chede told her. He watched her stiff upper lip begin to tremble.

Then he began to counsel her as he had so many others, saying, "You will need our services. This is not the end of your life."

● ● ●

Chede's story includes much more, but this is all that he felt comfortable telling me for this book. He even asked that I alter a few details to hide his identity because he worries that people will stigmatize his children. I am glad that there are adults, like Faith Alive support group leader Kate, who lavish love on children regardless of their families' HIV status.

Playing Games

I will not leave you as orphans; I will come to you.

John 14:18

2009

"Ready. Set. Go!" said Headmistress Kate. The precious five-year-old Nigerian girls jumped from their child-sized wooden chairs, picked up their battered backpacks, and began. The four girls each represented a different school team's color for Sports Day at Elim Elementary School in Jos, Nigeria. The contest: to see which of them could put on a school uniform, over her clothes, by herself. The winning title went not to the one who finished first but the one who dressed the smartest. All buttons in a row, bright pink shirts tucked under dark blue smocks, sandals buckled, backpacks zipped, and straps straightened.

The older children, resting after relay competitions, congregated on the dirt playground. They burst into cheers for their teams.

"Go, red team! Good job!" shouted those wearing red shorts and shirts.

"Keep going, green team!" shouted those wearing green.

"Yellow! Yellow!"

"Blue!"

The young contestants beamed with pride while trying to live up to expectations. Having this much attention and focus from 160 of their schoolmates, headmistress, and thirteen teachers was an honor.

The four girls pulled white socks over their dry feet, lifted their cotton shirts over their shortly cropped or braided hair, and buttoned their smocks. Even the bright morning sun beaming on the dust-blown playground seemed to encourage them to do their best.

Kate calmly balanced a teacher's toddler on her hip while she watched the children, some of whom were orphans and needed to learn how to dress themselves for school. A few of her students receiving scholarships also benefitted from health care at Faith Alive where she volunteered as a support group leader for people living with HIV.

"Ah," Kate said as she smiled down at the first girl to finish. The young student stood proud and erect as if at military attention. "Well done, Faith." Kate turned toward the other girls, now finishing, and said, "You are each so smartly dressed. Well done."

When the girls ran off to get their snacks, Kate's mind flashed back to when she had played games as a child.

In late 1966, five-year-old Kate had hidden behind the mango tree and waited. Would her brothers and sisters find her?

"Ready or not, here we come!" they had shouted. Kate heard the leaves rustle as the children sprang from the ground to seek her. Within a minute, one of her older brothers rushed around the tree and triumphantly yelled, "Found her!"

Kate wondered how her brother knew that she always hid there.

Just then, they heard their mum's voice summon them inside. Kate linked arms with one of her sisters while they skipped into their living room and sat down. Seeing her mum's empty lap, Kate jumped onto it as their daddy started to talk.

"My children," he said, "I have something important to say. You have been playing, but it is now time for us to be serious. There is talk of things…of possible trouble." He spoke generally, not yet having a name for the upcoming Biafran civil war in Nigeria. "Life will get more difficult, and we need to make some changes. I have been praying, and it might be best if some of you go to stay with relatives for a while because…"

Kate did not hear his explanation. She only saw his mouth moving. Moving. Would she have to go away from her parents? Something felt strange. She had heard her daddy listen to the serious voices on the radio and seen her mum crying. Kate's stomach growled because there had not been much food at dinner. She burrowed closer to the comfort of her mum's heartbeat.

Within months, Kate's aunt came to collect Kate. Crying, she looked up to her parents.

"It is okay," they assured her. "God willing, we will be together soon." They kissed their fifth child and said, "Be a big girl for your auntie and help her. She will make sure that you go to school...and whenever you miss us, pray to your Father in heaven for comfort."

Kate reluctantly followed her mum's junior sister while three other siblings went to live with other relatives. Only four stayed behind with their parents—the baby still breastfeeding, the next youngest, and the two oldest children. Kate's knobby knees soon cracked from being on her knees so often in prayer.

Things got much worse before they got better. By 1968, Kate's father died of a heart attack. Left to provide for the children, Kate's widowed and grieving mum injured her leg while trekking a long distance to find food. One dreadful night, the opposition attacked their house. Kate's four brothers and sisters tried unsuccessfully to resist. Only their mum survived, probably because, in her injured position, she did not pose a threat.

When Kate and her aunt heard the news, they wailed. *Dear, God,* Kate prayed between sobs, *I want my mum and daddy!* Her aunt's arms did not make her pain disappear like her mum's hugs had.

Seven-year-old Kate buried her mind in school, quickly becoming one of the top students. Not until she was in secondary school did God answer her prayers to be with her mum. It took that long for her mum to be in a position to provide for Kate. Also, Kate's mum needed her to help earn money. The five remaining family members, now reunited, all struggled to help. They walked to and from their mum's shop to the street, carrying pumpkin and bitter leaves for soup and carefully balancing the white plastic trays, filled with oranges, on their heads.

Years passed. Hungry as much for a man's attention as for food, Kate married and had two children before her twentieth birthday. She named her son Augustine, or Onyeka, meaning "Nobody's greater than God," and she named her daughter Elsie, or Oluchi, meaning "God's work."

Eager to continue her studies, Kate submitted an application for a university degree program in education. She heard about a scholarship at the same time she learned about her husband's wandering affections. He soon left her for another woman. As is a customary in Nigeria, her ex-husband and his parents had the power to keep the children. They chose to do so.

"My babies," Kate cried to her mum. "They are too young for me to give them advice like you did with me. They need to feel my mother-love."

Kate's mum, having endured many years of hardship, helped Kate face her new circumstances.

"Okay," her mum said, "if that is the situation, the problem is how do you continue your life?"

Strengthened by her mum's resolve and example, Kate busied her mind with university studies and eventually teaching jobs. But the nights did not provide a distraction. She wept and prayed for her children every night. She awoke from sleep to reach for them but, like phantom limbs, they were not there.

She tried over the next few years to visit her son and daughter, only to be denied. After her ex-husband remarried for the first and then the second time, Kate had to accept that other women were raising her children.

Abba, Daddy God, why can I not have my children? What life is there for a childless mother? It is as unnatural as calling something a living heart that has no blood pumping through it. I cannot bear this. I do not feel like my traditional name, Ogochukwu, God's favor.

Kate had no choice but to bear the pain until the late 1980s when God answered her prayers favorably. Her former in-laws finally allowed Kate to visit. Her soul filled with hope at reuniting with her beloved son and daughter. She saw them and knew—their developing bodies did not disguise the fruit of her womb. They looked at her, however, like a stranger, and addressed her as they would any other woman older than them.

"Hello, Auntie," they said as her fragile heart shattered.

Give me strength, Father God, and let them learn that I am their mum. I know how painful it is to not live with parents.

Kate persevered. Around 1990, she heard that her ex-husband had divorced his wife. So Kate contacted her former in-laws; they agreed to let her travel with her children. She collected her now nine- and seven-year-old children for Christmas break and took them to visit her side of the family. Surrounded by such love and happiness, the children realized that this woman was more than an auntie.

One day in Kate's mother's kitchen, Kate thought she heard Elsie's quiet voice from the next room say, "Mommy?" Kate walked slowly to the doorway, took a deep breath, and peered into the parlor. She saw Elsie sitting on a chair, looking directly at Kate.

"Did you say something?" Kate asked Elsie.

"Yes," Elsie said. "I said, 'Mommy.'"

Kate took another deep breath before she asked, "Were you talking to me?"

Elsie looked down at her lap and said, "Yes?"

Before Elsie could look up, Kate had rushed to Elsie's side, hugging her through tears of joy.

"Yes, yes, yes," Kate said. "I am your mum, and you are my daughter. I love you so very much. Yes, you are mine."

Elsie also wept, embracing the woman she had hoped was her real mother. Elsie would share the news with her brother as soon as he came inside from playing. But for now, she wanted their mother all to herself.

Kate would have to wait until her children were young adults before they were allowed to live with her. In the meantime, thirty-three-year-old Kate met Clement Iornongu, a full-time lawyer, part-time pastor, and single father of two elementary-school-aged boys. After spending time together in 1994, he said to her, "Your story kind of agrees with mine. You have two kids; I have two kids. We want to serve God fully. Join me to serve God as husband and wife."

Sensing God's hand in this offer, Kate changed her last name to her husband's first name and started answering to his pet name for her: Oninye, gift from God.

All Glory to you, oh Father, but how can I cope with other people's children when I long to be with my own? If you give me the challenge, though, I take it and will treat them as I want my children to be treated. To you be the glory.

She resigned her teaching job because their church discouraged Kate from paid work outside the home. With time spent at home, she noticed that many of the neighborhood children spoke only the tribal Hausa. They were not learning English, the official Nigerian language, so she began helping three or four of them with homework.

Kate considered this just a game, but the children's parents took notice. Their children's grades improved so dramatically that they offered much thanks. This gave her an idea to make her teaching more structured. In 1998, she took her small amount of personal life savings to the market, purchased a couple of small, wooden student desks and chairs, and set up a classroom in her home.

On the way to buy school supplies early one evening, she walked down Tafawa Balewa Street in Jos. She spotted a sign that read, "Faith Alive Counseling Center."

Hmm. God, what do they mean? What is this all about?

Reminded of her fulfilling experience as a Bible school counselor years earlier, she climbed the steps of the original Faith Alive building. As she walked through an open door, she heard the familiar swish,

swish, swish of a broom and saw the hunched back of a man sweeping.

"Excuse me," Kate said to him.

He turned around, quickly put down the broom, and said, "Yes, yes. You are welcome."

"I was just passing by and saw the sign. May I talk to someone about this Faith Alive?"

Expecting for the man to fetch someone in charge, Kate was surprised to see this worker motion for her to sit in the chair beside the desk while he sat behind it.

"You can talk with me," he said. "I am Dr. Isichei, but most people call me Dr. Chris."

Kate introduced herself and asked what he did at this counseling center.

"God asked me to start this about two years ago to help the poor, to present the gospel of Jesus Christ through holistic services," he said. "A few others have joined me in this ministry, some doctors and nurses and students who also volunteer. We started with counseling and have added other services, but we always offer prayers."

Struck by the simple yet profound message from this humble doctor, Kate told him about her previous counseling experience. She asked if she could volunteer at Faith Alive.

"Yes, yes!" he said. "Thank you so much. God will surely bless you."

As they worked out some details, Dr. Chris kept saying, "Thank you."

With her husband's blessing, she started going to Faith Alive on Thursday and Saturday evenings. Dr.

Chris asked Kate to chat with patients before or after they saw him or any of the handful of other doctors. While all the doctors were helpful, she soon noticed that most patients requested Dr. Chris because he treated them more like a close family member than a patient. While they came to him for help, he offered them hope.

One day in 2000, Dr. Chris came to her home. "Kate," he said, "we have started a support group on Sunday afternoons for HIV-positive patients, many of them widows. Medicine and counseling are not enough. They need to be encouraged, to learn, and to know that they are not alone."

"Yes, I agree," she said.

"I need a team of leaders for this, and you have a good relationship with many of our patients. You are gentle with them and always wanting to serve, even giving out of your own pocket. Will you please help?"

Kate respected him so much that if he believed in something, she knew it was special. Instead of taking her usual time to thoroughly think things through, she answered, "Yes, I will."

The Sunday afternoon group began with just a few women who gathered to sing and pray. Kate loved them and saw them not as victims of rapidly approaching death, but precious children of God. They soon called her Mama. Nurturing them filled a void while she waited for her own children to become adults when they could be together.

Within a few years, the support group grew from a handful of women to hundreds of men and women.

They shared encouragement, education, praise, testimonies, and games. "Ah," she told her husband one night at dinnertime, "Faith Alive is becoming a name to be reckoned with in Jos."

Support group members brought their children, some infected with HIV. Seeing the need for the parents to not be distracted during group time, Kate began taking their kids into another room where she read storybooks to them and played. This eventually turned into an official Kiddies Club at Faith Alive run by a group of young, energetic staff members. Like a mini vacation Bible school, each week they sang praise songs, played games, and learned about healthy living habits.

Back at home in 2000, Kate's classes had grown. What she had started as a game with just seven neighborhood children had increased to ten, then fifteen, then twenty boys and girls. Kate started to group them into ability levels. Not able to give them each the attention they craved, she started charging the parents a small token of money to hire a teacher. By the end of the year, the children and desks filled every part of her home.

God, what will you have me to do? I want to help these children, but we are running out of space. Lead me, Father God.

To make their home an officially licensed school, she and her husband decided to move to a different house. Their former home served as the school until enrollment increased to fifty students and five teachers.

With her husband's support, Kate then found a small building hidden off a main street and tucked at the base of some large rocks. She named her new school Elim after a resting spot for the Israelites on their exodus from Egypt. After days in the desert, the struggling Israelites came to an oasis with water wells and date trees. Yes, this school would provide nourishment for children's minds and souls as they journeyed from childhood to adulthood.

After settling into the new building, Elim offered classes through grade six. With parents' encouragement, Kate hoped to expand the school through grade twelve. She continued to invest all the money into the school and staff, taking no salary for herself.

● ● ●

God answered her prayer for a quality Christian school that is known beyond the walls of Nigeria. That happened because Sally Barlow from Albuquerque started a scholarship program for orphans and vulnerable children (OVCs) at Elim. In 2008, First Presbyterian Church in Fort Collins, Colorado, took over the scholarship leadership.

Kate told me that her dream is to move her family into a larger home—for two reasons. The first is that her daughter, Elsie, now lives with her, teaches part-time at Elim, and attends university. Her son, Augustine, occasionally stays with them and hopes to become a pastor. The other reason is that Kate wants their home to be an orphanage for OVCs, some of whom are patients at Faith Alive. Perhaps with Dr. Chris's wife, Dr. Mercy, as an Elim board member, they will find a way.

In the meantime, Kate and some of the teachers rotate which OVCs to take to a special home-away-from-home on the weekends. One of those times, Kate and her daughter, Elsie, took about twenty OVCs from Elim on a special picnic at local Shere Hills. After eating biscuits and jollof rice and sipping fruit drinks, the children grew restless.

"Let's play a game!" Elsie said. "Who wants to play follow the leader?"

Dozens of hands raised toward the blue sky. After Elsie appointed an older girl, the children followed their classmate over the hilly ground. They stood on tiptoes, stretched to the sky, and ran up and down the hills.

Kate smiled as she watched her daughter interact with the children.

Thank you, Father God, that you are faithful and do not leave us as orphans. Like the Bible says, you have dressed each of us with your armor. We have the belt of truth buckled around our waist and wear the helmet of salvation. Thank you for being our heavenly Father. We will continue to follow you as our leader. Amen.

Kate and others at Faith Alive follow Dr. Chris's example to help others at the weekly HIV support group meetings, one person at a time.

One by One

1984

Ogbonna Chinasa's skinny eight-year-old body nestled close to the wall on the small, lumpy mattress. She woke to the sound of tin pots and pans clinking in the kitchen and knew that it must be 3:00 a.m.—again.

She rubbed her eyes while pushing herself to a standing position and shuffled toward the kitchen. Nnamdi, her brother, fetched the large, tin pot of black-eyed peas that had soaked in water overnight. Auntie lit a candle even though Ogbonna and Nnamdi could skin each and every soft bean by feel. Ogbonna preferred the darkness so that she would not see how many thousands of beans waited in their pile for the next few hours. The moi moi had to be ready by 7:00 a.m. for Auntie to sell at the local market.

"Cut the red peppers and onions today, Ogbonna," said Auntie. Ogbonna's shoulders sagged. Arguing was no use, even if she had the energy, so she started mincing. Within a few minutes, she squinted her eyes in an attempt to fight the onion's sting. With closed eyes, memories flashed before her.

Daddy's rugged, protective arms cradling me, she remembered, as he reached down to hug me at the end of the day. Mama in her orange, yellow, and blue wrap brightening the kitchen as we made egusi soup. My sisters and brother played checkers with tin bottle caps. The joy of a new sunrise, all of us together, our morning routine singing praises to God.

"Yiii!" She had done it again. The knife pierced her sweet memories as blood rushed from her left palm.

"I am sorry, I am sorry," Nnamdi said as Nigerians typically do when anything bad happens. Auntie must have stepped outside, so Nnamdi quickly wrapped Ogbonna's hand in a nearby towel.

"Shh, shh now," Nnamdi said as he quietly traded jobs with his sister. No need to bring this to Auntie's attention; she would scold Ogbonna again for being such a clumsy girl.

Mama would have given me a kiss. I wish she were here. Oh, God, why did Daddy have to die from those hiccups? When will Mama come back and get us? When will she be done with what Auntie calls grieving? I do not want to live here and go to school. I just want my mama.

The thoughts pained her, so Ogbonna kept her eyes open during the next few hours of peeling and mashing beans. As she added the peppers, onion, spices, salt, and red palm oil, she saw the sunlight creep through the window curtain.

Nnamdi scooped the blended mixture into recycled tin cans, filling them about half full. Ogbonna poured a little water into a pot and stacked a dozen or so gray stones on the bottom where the tins of moi moi would steam bake. Today, Nnamdi would stay close to the fire and add water as it evaporated.

Ogbonna began sweeping, washing dishes, and fetching water from the river. She and her brother never considered sampling the moi moi. They knew it was for sale, and the income went to pay for their school fees. A stale piece of bread would have to be enough for this morning. Maybe even for this day.

After breakfast, the children walked down a dusty road to school. Holding only one or two pieces of paper and a pencil nub, their book bags hugged their bony backs. Once again they would watch other children eat lunch. They would try not to fall asleep during the lesson while their stomachs growled.

"Watch out!" Nnamdi cried. He pulled Ogbonna close to him, away from cars and motorbikes that swerved around potholes in front of them. Dodging danger had become their daily routine since their daddy had died a few months earlier.

1984 proved to be a rigorous and tedious year for them—work in the morning, school during the day, and more work in the evening. Before the sun set, they had to put new beans in the pot to soak before they crawled onto their mattress.

The dreaded routine continued until one day when Ogbonna and Nnamdi returned from school. Auntie bustled around tidying the house and washing the laundry, chores usually relegated to the children. Ogbonna sensed something different but did not understand what or why.

"Do your schoolwork, children," Auntie said. "Hurry! We need to be ready when your mama arrives."

Wait, did she say, 'when Mama arrives'?

Without thinking, Ogbonna darted out the door.

"Mama? Mama?" she called.

She looked down the road, past the neighbors.

"Ogbonna, you get in here right now," Auntie said, chasing after her. Auntie's swift hand barely missed Ogbonna's head as she darted down the street. Knowing that her mama was coming gave Ogbonna a boldness she did not know she possessed. Her lanky legs gathered speed as she snaked between storefronts. Confident that Auntie's swishing thighs could not carry her hefty body very quickly, Ogbonna hid behind a shabby green door. After a few minutes, she dared to peer around. She saw Auntie heading home, breathing heavily in defeat.

Ogbonna's hiding place served as a perfect vantage point—the town's main entry. She waited there for her mama. The sky got darker as the small street-side fires burned the day's trash. Every half hour or so, Ogbonna heard Auntie call out, "Ogbonna, Ogbonna, you get back here, girl." But Ogbonna did not care. She would wait here for her mama, even if it took forever. The open storefront felt safer than Auntie's loveless house.

Ogbonna tried to keep her eyes open as time passed. Her eyelids felt like cement. Just when she lost strength to hold them open any longer, she heard footsteps approaching.

Could it be? God, please let that be my mama.

Ogbonna lifted her eyelids and saw a familiar silhouette walking toward Auntie's house. Ogbonna leapt to her feet and sprinted toward her mama. Even in the near darkness, they recognized each other.

"Oh, Ogbonna, dear Ogbonna, I have missed you so," cried Mama, dropping her bulging bag on the dirt street. "I could not stay away from you any longer."

"Oh, Mama," said Ogbonna, tears rolling down her cheeks. "Don't leave me. Don't ever leave me again." Ogbonna hugged her mama's waist and leaned into her bosom.

"I will not, my dear," said Mama as she embraced Ogbonna. "We will find a way together."

They stayed attached for a few minutes before Mama asked, "Are you together with Nnamdi? Let us go collect him also."

Mama picked up her bag and they walked as one to Auntie's house. She whispered to Ogbonna, "God will give us a way. He will be our Father, our provider. I know a way to earn money so that we can all live together again."

After a tearful reunion with Nnamdi, Auntie invited Mama to sleep there that night. Mama, Ogbonna, and Nnamdi slept together like a loving mama dog and her pile of contented puppies on a mattress.

Before falling asleep, Mama prayed aloud, "Thank you, God. Our name, Chinasa, has come true. 'God answers.'"

They awoke the next morning to the smell of eggs.

At breakfast, Mama said, "Auntie, you have been so kind to take care of my children."

The siblings cast down their eyes but sat still.

"I wish there were some way that I could pay you," Mama continued. "But sadly, there is not. Please do accept my gift of these yams."

Mama lifted the brown bag and pulled out four large, lumpy yams. The children's eyes widened as they saw the log-like roots, big enough to feed Auntie for at least a week.

"Dalu," Auntie said in thanks. "These are very fine yams." Then she paused. She seemed to weigh the benefits of yams versus the children's labor. With a tsk, she said, "You have no idea how much I will miss the children's work."

After Mama and the children said their good-byes and left, Ogbonna asked Mama, "Will we have some yams, too?"

Mama smiled. "Oh yes, Ogbonna, we will have yams. We will have many yams."

From that day forward, they ate yams for nearly every meal. Mama never denied her children homegrown food. She had sold their furniture to invest in a yam business to provide income for her children. So many yams piled on their kitchen floor that Ogbonna often tripped over them. But she did not care. To her, yams meant comfort. Their flavor, no matter what spices her mama added, tasted like love.

That love served as a strong foundation as Ogbonna grew up, married, and had children. Her husband's diabetes prevented him from steady work at a car repair shop, so Ogbonna needed to find a job. In 2005, she did not have a degree; her mama had only been able to pay for one child to go to university, and it was not Ogbonna.

So her husband contacted his friend, Dr. Chris, at Faith Alive. She had heard that physical and metaphorical miracles happened at Faith Alive—people carried or wheeled in sometimes left on their own two legs. Dr. Chris appreciated her gentle, wise ways; he hired her for record keeping and then adherence counseling. She also often led morning devotions in the waiting room. Dr. Chris saw her genuine faith; she told people about Jesus because she knew him personally. He watched her pray with people, and he noticed how their countenance changed.

Dr. Chris needed someone he could trust to help care for patients in the evening hours after he worked all day at JUTH. That person would not just attend to the patients' physical needs, but also discern and feed their spiritual and emotional hungers. The evening schedule worked well for her because she began taking social work classes and studying during the day.

One evening, Dr. Chris sat in one of Faith Alive's small offices separated by an uninsulated wall from the waiting area where conversations competed with the small television's soap operas and cartoons. Ogbonna brought in a new patient and asked her to sit on a white plastic chair next to Dr. Chris at his desk.

After treating the woman, he said to the patient, "Ah, I see that your name is Dorcas. That is a biblical name. Are you a Christian?"

"Yes," she answered, as if this were an easy question.

"Wonderful!" Then he asked, "How do you know that you are a Christian?"

Tilting her head slightly, she said, "I go to church."

"Good. But even non-Christians can go to church. Is there another reason you know that you are a Christian?"

Pausing for a moment, she said, "I read the Bible."

"Excellent! But even non-Christians can read the Bible, can they not?"

The woman's head tilted the other direction. "I suppose so." She looked at Ogbonna sorting through a stack of files.

"Tell me then, so how do you know that you are a Christian?"

The woman cast her head down. She said nothing.

"You are friends with one of our staff members, yes?" he asked her.

The woman looked up and nodded. "Yes," she said.

"She is a Christian," he said. "Did she not tell you what it means to be a Christian? Did she not tell you about Jesus?"

"We do not talk about Jesus," Dorcas said.

"Oh no, that is not right. My friend, Ogbonna, she will tell you about Jesus."

Ogbonna looked up from the files.

"Yes, my friend, Ogbonna, will be your friend. She will take you and tell you about Jesus and how you can know that you are a Christian," Dr. Chris said as he smiled and gently placed his hand on her shoulder. "I want you to tell me about that the next time that you see me."

With that, Ogbonna gently led Dorcas into another room.

● ● ●

The following year, I watched Ogbonna with patients. She now sat behind the desk when people needed Dr. Chris in other parts of the hospital. In her purse under the desk, she carried a small container of cooked yams that she had made for one of the staff whose mother had just died. She also had some fresh cashews in a plastic bag. She offered some to me.

About that time, a nurse walked into the office and reached for the bag. Apparently, the staff knew where to look for food. Maybe Ogbonna's ample figure tipped them off, or maybe it was her past generosity.

As we waited for the next patient, I wondered how much Ogbonna knew about medicine. "Ogbonna, what will you do if one of the patients today needs to see Dr. Chris?"

"I will go and get him," she said. "But most of the time, they just need to pick up their prescriptions. I will check their weight and ask about their health. Not all of their problems will be medical. Many are hungry for something else—maybe love or happiness or forgiveness." She paused and then said, "You see this sign on the wall?"

I looked and saw a white paper with green lettering. It said, "Not what came before, but what next to do." I had to read it a few times slowly to understand that it meant people need to focus on the future and suspend judgment of the past.

"See," Ogbonna said in a soft voice, "many times people are troubled by what they have done in the past. Maybe that is even how they got sick. It is that guilt and shame that is making them feel sicker."

I nodded at Ogbonna's wisdom.

"You see, they need to know that God loves them for who they are, not for what they have done or not done. We are not here to ask questions about their past or to judge them. We are here to let them know about God's grace so that they can move forward. Not all sickness is in their bodies—sometimes it is in their souls. Do you understand what I am saying?"

"Yes," I said, "I do."

I also understand why Dr. Chris trusts Ogbonna to see his patients. She is a good friend who talks about Jesus, the one who nourishes and heals us. Sometimes she uses words. Other times, yams and cashews are enough.

I wondered what I could offer to people in need. And then I learned that a Faith Alive staff person's son suffered from a life-threatening heart condition.

Heartbeat of Hope

I will praise you, LORD, with all my heart...for your unfailing love and your faithfulness...

Psalm 138:1 & 2 excerpts

Throughout this book, I recreated the dialogue and actions based on accounts told to me by some of the faithful Nigerians I met during my journeys to Jos. With little Chris, however, God gave me a role in the story.

October 2006

Daniel, dressed in freshly pressed slacks and a button-down shirt, confidently led the generational trio into the northern Nigerian government hospital. Behind him walked his mother-in-law, carrying his first-born child. He was a son, no less, a namesake of two crucial role models: his father Mwajim, meaning "walking together," and Dr. Chris, the husband of Daniel's childhood neighbor in Maiduguri. Daniel and his wife, Rahila, had witnessed the compassionate doctor and his wife, Mercy, time and again offer help to strangers in this country where people struggled to provide for their own families.

"By God's grace," he had told his bride after their wedding a year earlier, "I would like to name our first child after such wonderful people. A boy will be Christian or a girl will be Mercy."

Rahila's smile lifted her full, shiny cheekbones in agreement.

Before their first anniversary, a baby grew in the safety of her womb. However, a taxi motorbike accident left seven-month-pregnant Rahila shaken and bleeding. A doctor delivered the boy successfully by emergency cesarean section five weeks earlier than nature intended.

This day, the proud Daniel and his mother-in-law transported the baby via motorbike to a government hospital for a routine six-week checkup while Rahila recovered at home. The grandmother safely cradled her grandson close to her heart while Daniel carefully navigated the dirt roads. Once at the hospital, she would help this new father settle the baby's cries.

"Sannu," Daniel greeted the hospital staff as the threesome entered the hospital. "How is work?" he asked a young man walking by wearing a white lab coat. As if ushering in the sunshine, he turned to a frowning, middle-aged admissions clerk and said, "It is a good day."

The clerk shifted her hefty weight on the chair and raised her head to look at this optimistic man. She pointed to the sign-in sheet. He took the pencil and wrote "Christian Mshelia Mwajim" before sitting on a bench next to his wife's mother in the quiet, dimly lit waiting room.

After engaging in lively conversation with a handful of people he recognized from living about thirty years in Maiduguri, Daniel heard a nurse call his son's name. Daniel held his head high as he took his small but priceless heir from his mother-in-law. The father and son entered the government doctor's office. After polite greetings, Daniel answered questions about Rahila's health.

"Your son," the doctor said after looking at little Chris, "he is small. But that is to be expected for a baby who entered the daylight early." The doctor reached for the baby and looked at his eyes, nose, mouth, and ears before putting a well-worn stethoscope on his chest. When Daniel noticed the doctor's brow furrow, he assumed that the doctor had difficulty hearing clearly.

"Um, hmmm," the doctor said, moving the stethoscope to another part of little Chris's chest. The doctor wrote something in the file. Daniel tried to see the words but could not because the doctor's arm blocked the view.

"I want you to listen to this," the doctor told Daniel as he passed him the stethoscope.

Daniel put the rubber-tipped ends into his ears and gently placed the round part on his son's chest. "Lub-*dup*...Lub-*dup*.......Lub-*dup*....Lub-*dup*..Lub-

dup," he heard mixed with something that sounded like water rushing through a hose.

"I do not understand," Daniel said. "Is this normal?"

"No," the doctor said, "I think there may be a problem. The thump is not regular." Looking at Daniel's raised eyebrows, the doctor asked, "Did you also hear that whishing sound?"

"Yes," Daniel said softly. "I think so."

"There are many things that might cause this murmur in your son's heart, but it would take much money to run tests to see what exactly is the problem."

Daniel's parted lips widened into an O as he exhaled. He, a recent college graduate, did not make enough money at a publishing company to provide for his wife plus thirteen younger brothers and sisters who relied on him. And now he had this baby. He already owed family and friends who contributed to the cost of his wife's recent cesarean surgery.

Sensing Daniel's hesitation, the doctor added, "Your son's heart problem might go away on its own, but I think that there is probably a hole in his heart. Even if we did the tests, there is nothing that we can do here for that problem."

Daniel worded his question carefully, starting to feel the weight of the possible answer. "If this is such a problem…and no medicine can help…what happens?"

"Your child," the doctor said slowly, "will not survive much."

Not survive. Not survive. Not survive. Heart. Murmur. Much money. Not survive. Not survive. Not survive. Oh my God. My God. What am I to do? Oh my God…

"Your son looks fine for now," the doctor reassured the distraught father, "and I am not sure about my diagnosis. Maybe," he added, "maybe I am wrong."

"Thank you, Doctor," Daniel said, steadying himself against the chair to stand. "I pray that you are. I will take him home now and love him for the time that God grants us."

Walking out of the hospital, the three silently mounted another motorbike. Each bump in the road on the way home could not jar Daniel out of his worries. How could he tell his wife in a way that would not weaken her recovering body or irreversibly pierce her soul? He knew, though, that she needed to know. They would shoulder the burden together. Besides, their son needed both of them to pray fervently.

So pray they did, at all hours of the day and night, revealing the fears that they dared not breathe aloud to others. Like many Nigerians, they did not freely share their problems because so many others also suffered.

Oh Lord, why have you given us this child only to take him away? Are you not faithful? How are we to face this? Give us strength. Make a way where there is no way.

Little Chris continued to seem healthy until the next spring when he clocked almost eight months. His parents began noticing their son's labored breathing and compared his small stature with other babies' growing bodies. His bright smile could not hide his face's blue tint.

About that time, Dr. Chris offered Daniel a position at Faith Alive. "We need someone to manage our storeroom," Dr. Chris said. "It is where we keep account of supplies and medications. We might not be able to pay more than you are earning already, but we are like family here. We are also starting a youth football team and need some coaches."

Without skipping a beat, Daniel accepted the offer. The family of three quickly moved to an apartment in Jos near Faith Alive. Daniel's jovial nature drew staff into the storeroom for supplies and smiles. He did not want to burden them with his problems, so many of them did not know the fear and trouble behind his smile and outward optimism. Besides, his son's diagnosis would only elicit disheartening pity in this country where most people die without access to specialized medical care.

Daniel's fears intensified with time. He knew that he must do whatever he could to save his son's life. So he bravely approached Dr. Chris at the hospital one day with little Chris.

"Ah, how is your son?" Dr. Chris asked.

"Doctor," Daniel said. "There is a problem with his heart, and we do not know what to do."

"Let me see," Dr. Chris said, taking the baby from Daniel and feeling for his pulse. After finding it, he said, "I see. I see. I am not a heart doctor, but I serve on the board of HeartAid, a place that helps children with heart problems."

"I am listening, yes," said Daniel eagerly.

"Go there," Dr. Chris instructed. "Yes, go there, and see if they can help. They cannot help everyone, but they will know what to do."

Then he added, "We will sort it out. Leave it to God, and He will definitely have a way. Believe in God."

"Thank you," Daniel said, "Sir, I am most grateful. May God richly reward you."

That week, Daniel and Rahila took little Chris to HeartAid, a non-profit in Jos. The doctors there did some tests free of charge and diagnosed him with not only a hole in the heart, but also a malposition of the great arteries—a serious complication.

"This is something that we cannot fix in Nigeria," the young HeartAid doctor said. "We do not yet have the equipment or the training for heart surgery in this country. We wait for people to donate money to send some children to India or America for surgery. But there is a waiting list. A long list."

"But it could happen?" Daniel said as a mixture of statement and question.

"Perhaps," the doctor said. "Perhaps...but it would take a miracle."

That same evening, Daniel and Rahila prayed together.

God, in the name of Jesus, we ask for a miracle.

When Daniel returned to Dr. Chris the next day to share the pediatric cardiologist's report, Dr. Chris said, "Do not worry. If it is God's will, it will happen. Just wait and see what God will do." Looking at the distraught young father, he added, "Leave it in his hands. He will definitely surprise us."

During his next few years, little Chris grew more slowly than other children his age. But his stunted growth did not interfere with his intelligence. By three years of age, he sang his ABCs and recited ascending numbers at preschool where he received top marks. His parents beamed with pride, treasuring each birthday and milestone as if it might be his last.

At Faith Alive, Daniel continued to work in the storeroom, coach football, take his turn leading morning devotions and afternoon prayers, and greeting international guests. He remembered Dr. Chris's words to the staff to not to burden visitors with personal problems. When visitors came, he did not mention his son's heart problems.

Daniel did not mention it, that is, until I returned home after my second visit to Faith Alive. He and I became Facebook friends, and I casually asked questions about his family. When he said that his son did not feel well, I asked probing questions.

"My son has a serious heart condition and often falls ill," Daniel said.

"Oh, Daniel, I'm sorry," I said. "I'll pray for your family."

Later that week, I showed photos of my recent Nigeria trip to Nanci Sebeneicher, a Save-A-Life sponsor visiting Colorado from Maryland.

"Oh," I said, pointing to a picture I had taken of Daniel holding little Chris. "It's so sad. I just learned that this little boy needs heart surgery, but he can't get it in Nigeria."

"I have a friend," Nanci said excitedly, "who helps children find heart surgeries in the United States. I'll bet she can help."

My jaw dropped and I said, "Praise God! See, miracles happen all the time for Faith Alive. I shouldn't be surprised." I shut the photo album and thought that it was a done deal. *Surgery, success, no problem.*

On my next trip to Nigeria a few months later, I happily played the role of Nanci's messenger. All I needed to do was get a written report from little Chris's doctor, send it to Nanci, and sit back to watch God work.

"Oh, here you are!" Daniel exclaimed when he saw me at Faith Alive. "The doctor is here to give you a report. Please, please, come with me to my office."

I dutifully followed Daniel to his third floor office where I sometimes used his painfully slow laptop—that is, if the generator purred or NEPA, the utility company, granted electricity. On a white plastic chair near rows of metal shelves lined with office supplies, bags of mosquito nets, and paper supplies, sat little Chris's HeartAid doctor.

"Please, please, meet Dr. Yilgwan," Daniel said, offering me a chair. "You must talk." Daniel pulled up a chair beside us and sat at the edge of his seat. After polite greetings, Dr. Yilgwan asked if I had seen his previous written report about little Chris.

I sensed Daniel's anxiety as he shuffled through the pile of papers on his lap. "Here," Daniel said, "let me get it. I have it. Right here. Just a moment, please, I have it. Please, please." In his uncharacteristic rush to provide the paper, everything on Daniel's lap dropped to the floor. Daniel hurriedly gathered the papers, fumbling a few times to find the report. "Please, please," he said.

At that moment, I realized the depth of this father's love for his son and how much he would do to provide for his flesh and blood. His desperation pierced my heart. Daniel, this man whom I had only seen up to this point as gregarious and fun-loving, whom my traveling team called "Handsome Daniel" to distinguish him from the other Daniels at Faith Alive, revealed his true identity—a scared and vulnerable daddy who said that he spent sleepless nights in anxiety and prayer.

"Here, here it is," he said, passing me the report—and the proverbial baton. I knew then that I would do whatever I could to help this father save his son.

After returning to Colorado, I immediately scanned and e-mailed the report to Nanci. Hoping to show Nanci the importance of helping little Chris get surgery, I said, "Let me know what I can do to help."

In an effort to prod Nanci to swift action, I added, "I'll do what it takes to see this surgery happen."

Nanci and I e-mailed back and forth over the next few months, even sharing the news that little Chris would soon be a senior brother. When Nanci's contacts did not produce anything and other commitments vied for her time, I took the lead. Nanci mentioned the Gift of Life International agency as a possibility, so I contacted them. Not knowing if the miracle would come quickly, I added little Chris to my church's prayer chain.

In January 2010, a violent crisis erupted in Jos followed by a strictly enforced curfew. Daniel and his family, like many people in Jos, did not feel safe to move about freely. Rahila's due date came and went. When her labor finally came, swift and frantic, they were unable to get her to the private hospital where prearrangements had been made for delivery. She delivered at Faith Alive.

Like an alarmingly high rate of Nigerian newborns, their daughter did not survive the birth journey. Her umbilical cord, the same thing that had sustained her life up to this point, created a deadly noose around her neck.

Daniel was speechless. He did not know what to tell his son about this baby sister.

"Christian, your baby is not here," Rahila soon told their son. "She is in heaven."

Seeing her son's disappointment, she added, "One day, you can play with her in heaven."

Overshadowed by the loss, Daniel and Rahila pressed on to find hope for their son. The Gift of Life International contact worked hard and provided a promising lead with a hospital in the United States. Confident that this was God's answer, I sent a digital EKG to the contact.

Daniel, Rahila, and I waited. And waited.

I e-mailed this contact every two weeks, making sure that the worker did not forget us. Deadlines for a "yes" came and went. In May 2010, this contact finally said, "My doctor connections say that little Chris will need at least two surgeries over the next ten to fifteen years. Even those will not cure his heart. No doctor in the United States wants to take this risk. There are hundreds of other children they can serve who have a better chance at survival. I'm sorry."

With that news, I reluctantly phoned Daniel. "Daniel. I don't know what else to do. My own efforts haven't produced a surgery. If this is going to happen, it'll only be by God's power. I'm powerless," I said as I choked back tears.

"It is okay. Okay," he reassured me in an unusual reversal of comfort.

After hanging up the phone, I sobbed and pleaded with God. *Do I just give up, God? Do I just sit back and let this dear boy die? I am available, but I have no earthly idea of what to do next. Surely this is not your will. Give me strength, Lord. Show me the way.*

Suddenly empowered with a fierce determination, I recommitted. If little Chris died, it would not be because I gave up. I was invested if God had another plan.

Shaking, I dialed Daniel's phone number.

"Hallo," Daniel said.

"Daniel," I said, "I don't know what God's plan is, but I will not give up. I think that God wants me to gather an army of people to help. I don't know who they are or what they'll do, but I need to recruit some people."

"Okay," he said, "whatever you think is best is the best. I have always said that."

"We will not give up hope," I assured him. "Pray for an army."

Over the next six weeks or so, I told Daniel that a number of people via Facebook wanted to help. While their contacts led to a flurry of new leads, none of them produced a plan. But they led to something else—an army of people praying, people who shared an investment in the outcome.

"How's little Chris?" my family asked me.

"What's the latest with little Chris?" my Facebook friends asked.

"We're praying for little Chris," people in my church's congregation said.

"Ah!" Daniel replied when I told him about this army. "My son is as well known in the United States as President Obama!"

During this time, Daniel connected me with Dr. Bode Thomas, the head of HeartAid in Jos. After a few e-mail exchanges, she told me about her contacts in Bangalore, India. The e-mails began to fly as we discovered that the total cost of surgery, including travel for Daniel and little Chris, would be $10,000. Finally, something concrete and much less than the expense of surgery in the United States.

Daniel and Rahila prayed. "Dear God, help them to get ten thousand dollars. We do not think that they have that kind of money available."

My husband, Mark, and I also prayed for God to show us a way. We never liked asking friends and family for money for our kids' myriad school and sports' fundraisers. But this was something far different, something worth the risk of alienating and indebting ourselves. We prayed before writing a personal plea, signing our names, and mailing the letters.

Money began pouring in. Soon, our donation plus people's $10 to $500s added up to $5,000. One friend, whose finances did not allow her to donate, felt convicted that the full amount had to be raised. That week, the friend talked to another church member who happened to be helping an elderly gentleman distribute some of his money. When that person told the man about little Chris, the man said, "Isn't that who we've been praying for in church? How much do you need?" He donated the last $5,000.

Awestruck at God's provision through my friends and family, in September 2010, Daniel packed and repeatedly rearranged his suitcase. With snack packs of his son's favorite cereal, Daniel and little Chris kissed Rahila good-bye. Not wanting to frighten her son, she waited until he wheeled his child-sized suitcase out of sight before releasing her flood of tears.

Due to time zones, the morning of the surgery in Bangalore, India, was the prior night in Colorado. Tossing and turning in bed, I got up to phone Daniel. Our telephone prayers bridged the gap between his waiting room and my kitchen. To keep his mind occupied, I asked him many questions about happy times in his life.

Daniel also called his wife who could not bring herself to eat anything until the surgery ended. He tried to comfort her crying but did not have the strength. They prayed during what seemed like the longest time of their lives. After hanging up, Daniel wandered the hospital halls until a security man told him to sit down.

Hours later, the surgeon walked into the waiting room. When he saw his patient's father, the surgeon said, "The surgery has gone well. However, the next few days will prove whether your son's heart will respond well—or not." He went on to explain about the tubes attached to little Chris's body before escorting Daniel to the pediatric intensive care room.

No warning could have prepared Daniel to see his son's body dwarfed by the tangle of endless wires. Little Chris breathed through something that looked like a space mask, and he wore a long gauge bandage down the center of his chest.

Oh God, is my son really alive?

Daniel walked softly and slowly over to his son.

"May I…may I touch him?" he whispered to the nurse.

"Very carefully," she said. "He will want to see you when he opens his eyes. There is a chair here for you."

Daniel sat, staring at his son, and waited. During the next few hours, Daniel watched nurses continually monitor little Chris until one of them said, "He is waking."

Daniel jumped from his chair and rushed to his son's side in time to see little Chris's eyes close again.

"He will come in and out of sleep for some time. There is a lot of medicine in his system," the nurse explained.

Daniel went back to his chair, alternating between jumping at the slightest noise or movement and sitting down to rest. But unlike his son, sleep did not come.

Little Chris recovered a little bit each day. Finally, the doctors saw that he was well enough and removed his breathing tube. After a few more weeks of highly supervised recovery in India, Daniel and his son once again boarded an airplane—this time for home.

Once in Jos, Rahila ran to greet them with hugs and kisses. Her firstborn, her son, was home again.

"Mommy!" he said. "I got a new toy! See!" He pulled the exercise toy out of his pocket.

"Wow!" she said as she lifted his shirt to examine his chest. Admiring his scar and putting one hand on her stomach, she said, "You have a lot of new things. Would you also like to have a new junior brother or sister?"

"Yes!" he declared with new strength. "Or a puppy!"

"Well, we do not have a puppy," she said, "but we will have another baby. And the two of you can run and play and grow up together."

As little Chris ran off to look for his Barney book, Daniel offered a prayer of thanksgiving with his wife.

"In Jesus' name, amen. Thank you, God, for making a way when there was no way. Thank you for our army of people praying and donors walking together. Thank you for my job at Faith Alive that has paid me so much more than a salary. You are so faithful. On behalf of our son, we praise you with all of our hearts."

Before long, Rahila had to lengthen her son's pants and shirtsleeves to accommodate his growth. She carefully washed and folded his outgrown clothes to save for her next child to be born in April 2011.

A sonogram revealed a healthy girl growing in her womb. Her pregnancy progressed well until her ninth month. She took a jolting fall in the bathroom. Rushing to the hospital, the doctors listened for the baby's heartbeat. All sounded well, and Rahila stayed a few days to make sure. She wanted to deliver naturally, if possible. The doctor sent her home with advice about monitoring the baby's heartbeat.

Resting and taking good care of herself, Rahila noticed that her baby's movements slowed. She checked the heartbeat often. Soon she heard no sound…and felt no more kicks. A visit to the hospital confirmed her worst fears.

She delivered naturally, saying hello and good-bye simultaneously to another daughter.

Because Faith Alive had recently started a cemetery, Daniel took his junior daughter to be buried there.

● ● ●

Little Chris continues to add weight and energy. It will be about ten years before teenaged Chris will need another surgery, possibly a heart transplant. Impossible? As of 2012, no hospital in Nigeria had the equipment or skill to handle this kind of delicate heart surgery. Could equipping Faith Alive Hospital for pediatric heart surgery be one of those God-sized goals that Dr. Chris mentions?

Faith Alive Invitation

What good is it, my brothers and sisters, if someone claims to have faith but has no deeds? Can such faith save them? Suppose a brother or a sister is without clothes and daily food. If one of you says to them, 'Go in peace; keep warm and well fed,' but does nothing about their physical needs, what good is it? In the same way, faith by itself, if it is not accompanied by action, is dead.

James 2:14-17

The large white banner at Faith Alive says, "Sannu da Zuwa" meaning, "You are welcome here." Everyone, regardless of tribe or tongue, is invited to become part of the extended Faith Alive family.

I once asked Dr. Chris about his greatest need at Faith Alive. Expecting to hear something about money or medications—both dire necessities—Dr. Chris's answer surprised me.

"Human resources," he said.

After pausing for a moment, I asked why.

"It is people we need most. All the money in the world does not help unless I have people to help bring visions into reality."

What Dr. Chris does not say, and maybe does not fully realize, is that we desperately need role models like him and the staff at Faith Alive who represent Christ to a needy world. We need to learn from them how to face and overcome obstacles, big or small, that threaten to drag us into a pit of doubt and despair. We need people like Dr. Chris and his staff to mentor us toward a faith in Jesus Christ that is fully alive.

If you have read this far in the book, then I believe that God might have a divine appointment for you. Are you ready to accept whatever invitation he might be extending to you at Faith Alive or elsewhere?

Faith in Action

You have limitless ways to put your faith into action for the thousands of Chiomas and Chedes who come to Faith Alive each month.

- Ask yourself, "AIDS: Am I Doing Something?"

- Pray about how God might want to match your unique gifts and talents with Faith Alive's immense needs.

- Schedule a minimum two-week vision or mission trip for yourself and/or a group of people. Helpful skills include medical, administrative, organizational management, teaching/training, counseling, pastoring, intercessory prayer, addiction recovery, mentoring, financial/accounting, computer, construction, writing, soccer, farming, sewing, knitting, and woodworking.

- Hold a fundraiser to collect money and medications to donate generally or for a specific need (children's health, educational scholarships, future Faith Alive teaching hospital, etc.).

- Purchase copies of this book to give to friends, family, neighbors, co-workers, employees, organizations, or congregations. All profit benefits Faith Alive Foundation-Nigeria.

- Go to www.faithalivenigeria.org and make a donation.

- Pray, individually or as a group, for God to touch more lives through Faith Alive.

- Educate your congregation or organization about Faith Alive or any issues raised in this book by hosting a Faith Alive speaker.

For more information, contact:

Erika Wiebe Nossokoff
International Coordinator
Faith Alive Foundation-Nigeria
http://erikanossokoff.tateauthor.com
www.faithalivenigeria.org
http://notesfromnigeria-erika.blogspot.com

Faith Formations: Discussion and Reflection Questions

Journey to Jos: How am I like or unlike the author whose fears almost stopped her from answering God's call to international missions? Reflect on Hebrews 11:1, "Now faith is confidence in what we hope for and assurance about what we do not see."

My Name is Christian: What does my name mean? What does it mean to carry a Christian identity? Would I stand for Christ, whatever the perceived cost?

Birthday in the Bush: Am I a threat to the devil? If not, why not? Would I be able to pray with and for people who harm me?

Coke Can: What negative thoughts and fears tempt to overtake me? What stops me from acting on Dr. Chris's exhortation to "go live my life" each day?

Godly Woman: How can I share my belongings and home with others in need?

Daddy's Legacies: What values am I instilling in my children? What can I learn from Dr. Chris's parenting style?

Connections: How do I respond when I find God offering me a surprise opportunity? How can I prepare myself for new relationships that God might want to use for future ministry?

God-Sized Goals: What is my God-sized goal? How might God want to use my little for big things?

Out of the Ashes: On a continuum with "Maundy/Holy Thursday" thinking on one end and "Resurrection Day" thinking on the other, where does my attitude fall? When have I seen God redeem a bad situation in my life or in someone else's life?

Architect for God: How have I been burned by life? What am I building for God?

Positive Pastor: What holds me back from feeling wholly loved and accepted by God's grace? How can I open that part of myself to receive his unconditional love?

Cinderella Revisited: How is my life like or different from a fairy tale?

Nurse with a Purse: Whom do I need to forgive? What would I pack in a bag if I knew it was all I could take if my home burned?

Pills under the Pillow: In what area of my life do I need God to intervene with his provision?

Righteous Reversal: Whom do I resent? What justice do I hope to see in my lifetime?

Playing Games: How might God use me in a leadership position to do something big for God? How am I equipping the next generation to love God?

One by One: What kind of Christian friend am I? How can I focus on "not what came before, but what next to come?"

Heartbeat of Hope: What spiritual heart issue in my life needs to be repaired? How might God want me to put my faith in action at Faith Alive or elsewhere?

To schedule an in-person presentation or virtual conversation with author Erika Wiebe Nossokoff for your church, small group, book club, or other gathering, contact her through http://erikanossokoff.tateauthor. com.

Faith Alive's Vision, Mission, Motto, and Dedication Declaration

Vision: Faith Alive Foundation envisions a self-sustaining, internationally recognized medical and social services center, which meets the needs of humanity in a holistic way.

Mission: To serve humanity by expressing God's love through compassionate voluntary services and the provision of free holistic health care and social services for improved quality of life.

Motto: Investing in and infecting lives for Jesus Christ our Savior.

Dedication Declaration: We have gathered to declare that we will refuse to settle for less than God's best! Therefore, we make the following affirmations:

I am confident in God's promises. My past has been forgiven. My future is secure and God has a purpose for my life.

I am committed to God's purposes. I will live my life serving God's purposes with God's power for God's glory. I will value character over comfort, service over status, and people over possessions.

I am committed to God's people. We declare that unity in Christ bridges all differences. We are one in Christ! Standing side by side with my brothers and sisters, I commit myself to grow spiritually, love unconditionally, and serve faithfully.

To my Lord and Savior Jesus Christ, I say: however, whenever, wherever, and whatever you ask me to do, my answer in advance is *yes!* I want to be used by you in such a way that on that final day I'll hear you say, "Well done, good and faithful servant!"

Faith Alive's Services

(offered free of charge to patients)

Adherence counseling
Business center
Café/Canteen
Celebrate Recovery (addictions)
Cemetery
Community trainings
Counseling
Daily devotions for staff and patients
Daily health talks for patients
Daycare for volunteers' children
Discipleship classes for skills-acquisition students
Doctor and nurse visits
Elementary school
Emergency room
FANOL bank (Faith Alive Necessities Of Life
    offering clothes, food, etc.)
Farmland
HIV awareness and education
HIV support group
Home-based care
In-patient care
Institute of Millennium Development Goals

Kiddies club (music, art, recreation, soccer, math, French)

Lab (including HIV testing)

Library

Mentoring classes

Micro-loans

Monthly spiritual themes

Nutrition unit offering FANOL paste (vitamin-enriched peanut butter)

Palliative care

Pediatric unit

Pharmacy

Prayer

Prenatal care and delivery

Recreation center

Rehabilitation for commercial sex workers

Salon for hair and nails

Satellite clinics in rural areas

School scholarships

Skills-acquisition classes (sewing, knitting, arts and crafts, computer, driving, catering)

Soccer teams for youth

Surgery (cesarean sections, prostrate, hernia, etc.)

Thrift shop

Transitional housing

Tuberculosis unit

X-rays and sonograms

Faith Alive's International Partners

- Association of Nigerian Physicians in the Americas (Leawood, Kansas)

- Bayside Covenant Church (Granite Bay and Folsom, California)

- Bethesda Baptist Church (Rochester, Minnesota)

- Christ Anglican Church (Ugboba, Issele-Uku, Delta State, Nigeria)

- Christian Health Association of Nigeria/ CHARIS (Nigeria)

- Church of the Nativity (Timonium, Maryland)

- Faith Alive USA, Inc. (Fort Collins, Colorado)

- First Presbyterian Church (Fort Collins, Colorado)

- First Presbyterian Church of Berkeley (Berkeley, California)

- Fowler Presbyterian Church (Fowler, California)

- Fresno First Baptist Church (Fresno, California)

- Global Strategies For HIV Prevention (Albany, California)

- Heart to Heart International (Olathe, Kansas)

- Hope for West Africa Foundation, Inc. (Lutherville, Maryland)

- Institute of Human Virology (Maryland and Nigeria)

- Immanuel Christian Reformed Church (Fort Collins, Colorado)

- LifeBridge Christian Church (Longmont, Colorado)

- Madera County Public Health Department (Madera, California)

- Mennonite Central Committee (United States, Canada)

- Mission Africa (Edinburgh, Scotland)

- Overseas Fellowship of Nigerian Christian Women (Birmingham, United Kingdom)

- Rochester Covenant Church (Rochester, Minnesota)

- St. Thomas of Canterbury Episcopal Church (Albuquerque, New Mexico)

- Tearfund (United Kingdom)

- The United States President's Emergency Plan for AIDS Relief (Washington, D.C.)

- United Baptist Church (Jos, Nigeria)

Any omissions are unintentional.

●　　●　　●

For those who are already part of the extended Faith Alive family, Dr. Chris offers his gratitude. "To my dear brothers and sisters, I want to thank you for making us feel the love of God. For making us know that we are one in Christ, irrespective of the distance, irrespective of the color, irrespective of the race. We are very appreciative. Thank you for investing in human lives, thank you for showing many the love of Jesus Christ.

I am sure that if Jesus were here, he would have sent you to do this on his behalf. Thank you for being sight to those who don't have sight. Thank you for being mind to those who don't have mind. Thank you for being feet to those who don't have feet. Thank you for being hands to those who don't have hands. Thank you for being good ambassadors of the Lord Jesus Christ. Thank you and God bless you."

Glossary

Animist: Belief that inanimate objects have spirits for good or evil

ARVs: Antiretroviral medications to treat, but not cure, HIV/AIDS

Baba: Daddy

Cassava: Large, yam-like root vegetable

CD4: Number of a person's T Cells indicating health; the higher the better

Chop: Eat, food

Dalu: Thank you in the Igbo/Ibo tribal language

FANOL Paste: Faith Alive Necessities of Life vitamin-enriched peanut butter

Handset: Cell phone

Hijab: Headscarf worn by some Muslim women to conceal their hair and neck

How now?: How are you?

Junior: Newer wife in polygamous marriage, or younger child

JUTH: Jos University Teaching Hospital

Kai: Utterance of disgust

Malta: Thick, malty, non-alcoholic beverage

Nagode: Thank you in Hausa language

Naira: Nigerian unit of money ($1 = n160)

NEPA: National Electric Power Authority in Nigeria

Offed: Turned off

Okada: Motorcycle taxi

OVCs: Orphans and vulnerable children

PEPFAR: President's Emergency Plan for AIDS Relief

Pounded Yam: Root vegetable like large tubular-shaped potatoes, not the same as Southern sweet potatoes

Ramadan: Islamic holiday when Muslims fast between dawn and dusk

Sannu: Hello in Hausa language

Sannu da zuwa: You are welcome, a greeting

Save-A-Life: Personal sponsorship program for HIV-positive patients

Senior: First wife in polygamous marriage, or older child

Snap, Snaps, Snapping: Photo, taking photos

Wrap: Fabric worn as a garment

Nigerian Statistics

Population: 158,423,000

Under-five mortality rate, 2010: 143 out of 1,000

Infant mortality rate (under 1), 2010: 88

Life expectancy at birth, 2010: 51 years

% of population using improved drinking water sources, 2008: 58

% of population using improved sanitation facilities, 2008: 32

Estimated adult (aged 15-49) HIV prevalence, (%) 2009: 3.6

Estimated number of people (all ages) living with HIV, 2009: 3,300,000

Prevention among young people (aged 15-24), % who have comprehensive knowledge of HIV, 2005-2010: (male 33%, female 22%)

Orphans, children (aged 0-17) orphaned by AIDS, 2009, estimate: 2,500,000

Orphans, children (aged 0-17) orphaned due to all causes, 2009, estimate, 12,000,000

Total adult literacy rate (%), 2005-2010: 61%

Number per 100 population, 2010, mobile phones: 55

Number per 100 population, 2010, internet users: 28

Primary school participation, net enrollment ratio (5), 2007-2010: (males 66%, females 60%)

Secondary school participation, net enrollment ratio (5), 2007-2010: (males 29%, females 22%)

% of population below international poverty line of US $1.25 per day, 2000-2009: 64%

Maternal mortality ratio, 2008, lifetime risk of maternal death: 1 in 23

Child marriage, 2000-2010, married by 15: 17

Child marriage, 2000-2010, married by 18: 39

Female genital mutilation/cutting, 1997-2010, attitudes, support for the practice: 22

Justification of wife beating, 2002-2010: (males 30, female 43)

Skilled attendant at birth (5), 2006-2010: (urban 65%, rural 28%)

Underweight prevalence in children under five (5), 2006-2010: (urban 16%, rural 27%)

(UNICEF, www.unicef.org/infobycountry/nigeria_ statistics.html as viewed on August 21, 2012)

Nigeria is Africa's largest producer of oil and the sixth largest oil producing country in the world. (Nigeria National Petroleum Corporation, http://www.nnpcgroup.com/NNPCBusiness/ UpstreamVentures/OilProduction.aspx)

Recommended Resources

Faith Alive's official website: www.faithalivenigeria.org.

Author's blog: *Notes from Nigeria,* http://notesfrom nigeria-erika.blogspot.com.

Author's website: http://erikanossokoff.tateauthor.com.

An African Awakening: My Journey into AIDS Activism by Valerie Bell, Authentic Books, 2007.

Cross-Cultural Servanthood: Serving the World in Christlike Humility by Duane Elmer, IVP Books, 2006.

Say Yes to God: A Call to Courageous Surrender by Kay Warren, Zondervan 2010.

Short-Term Missions Workbook: From Mission Tourists to Global Citizens by Tim Dearborn, IVP Books, 2003.

When Helping Hurts: Alleviating Poverty Without Hurting the Poor. . .and Yourself by Steve Corbett and Brian Fikkert, Moody Publishers, 2009.

Women, HIV and the Church: In Search of Refuge edited by Arthur J. Ammann and Julie Ponsford Holland, Cascade Books, 2012.